M. Bidoit   H.-J. Kreowski   P. Lescanne
F. Orejas   D. Sannella (Eds.)

Algebraic
System Specification
and Development

A Survey and Annotated Bibliography

Springer-Verlag

Berlin Heidelberg New York
London Paris Tokyo
Hong Kong Barcelona
Budapest

Series Editors

Gerhard Goos
GMD Forschungsstelle
Universität Karlsruhe
Vincenz-Priessnitz-Straße 1
W-7500 Karlsruhe, FRG

Juris Hartmanis
Department of Computer Science
Cornell University
Upson Hall
Ithaca, NY 14853, USA

Volume Editors

Michel Bidoit
LIENS, CNRS and Ecole Normale Supérieure
45, rue d'Ulm, F-75230 Paris Cedex 05, France

Hans-Jörg Kreowski
Fachbereich Mathematik und Informatik, Universität Bremen
Postfach 330440, W-2800 Bremen 33, FRG

Pierre Lescanne
CRIN and INRIA, Campus Scientifique
B. P. 239, F-54506 Vandoeuvre-les-Nancy, France

Fernando Orejas
Facultat d'Informàtica, Universitat Politècnica de Catalunya
Pau Gargallo, 5, 08028 Barcelona, Spain

Donald Sannella
Department of Computer Science, University of Edinburgh
Mayfield Road, Edinburgh, EH9 3JZ, Scotland

CR Subject Classification (1991): D.2.1.-2., D.2.4, D.2.6, D.2.10-m, D.3.1-3,
F.3.1-2, I.1

ISBN 3-540-54060-1 Springer-Verlag Berlin Heidelberg New York
ISBN 0-387-54060-1 Springer-Verlag New York Berlin Heidelberg

Printing and binding: Druckhaus Beltz, Hemsbach/Bergstr.
2145/3140-543210 - Printed on acid-free paper

Lecture Notes in Computer Science 501

Preface

Methods for the algebraic specification of abstract data types were proposed in the early seventies in the USA and Canada and became a major research issue in Europe shortly afterwards. Since then the algebraic approach has come to play a central role in research on formal program specification and development, as its range of applications was extended to the specification of complete software systems, to the formal description of the program development process, and to the uniform definition of syntax and semantics of programming languages. Today this approach extends beyond just software to the development of integrated hardware and software systems. These flourishing activities in the area of algebraic specifications have led to an abundance of approaches, theories and concepts, which have universal algebra, category theory and logic as a common mathematical basis.

The present volume is an annotated bibliography which attempts to provide an up-to-date overview of past and present work on algebraic specification. No attempt is made to provide a coherent introduction to the topic for beginners; the intention is rather to provide a guide to the current literature for researchers in algebraic specification and neighbouring fields. Some indications of how the different approaches are related are included, together with some ideas concerning possible future directions.

This volume arose out of the work of the COMPASS Basic Research Working Group, funded by the European Community under the Basic Research Action programme, ref. no. 3264 (see [Kri 90a], [KP 90]) and coordinated by Bernd Krieg-Brückner of the Universität Bremen. The name COMPASS stands for "a COMPrehensive Algebraic approach to System Specification and development". An early version of this document was included in the original COMPASS project proposal as a review of the state of the art [Kri 89a]. The current version is the result of suggestions for improvements from the participants in the COMPASS project, assembled and edited into a more or less coherent form by five editors. Since the COMPASS working group includes most of the leading European experts in algebraic specification, the result should be a relatively comprehensive overview of the main work in the field. But because of the somewhat haphazard way in which this volume arose, there are inevitable gaps and inaccuracies. We apologize for these in advance, and in particular to anybody whose work has inadvertently been omitted. In spite of its deficiencies, we hope that it nevertheless represents a useful snapshot of the current state of the art.

Acknowledgements

We thank those members of the COMPASS working group who contributed to the original grant proposal and/or who later submitted suggestions for improvements. The members of COMPASS are listed overleaf. Thanks also to Oliver Schoett for suggestions for improvement, and to Monika Lekuse for help with the editing. Special thanks to Bernd Krieg-Brückner for coordinating COMPASS.

The COMPASS Working Group

Universitat Politécnica de Catalunya, Barcelona: *Fernando Orejas*; Silvia Clérici, Marisa Navarro (San Sebastian), Roberto Nieuwenhuis, Pilar Nivela, Ricardo Peña, Vera Sacristan, Ana Sanchez (San Sebastian)

Technische Universität Berlin: *Hartmut Ehrig, Peter Pepper*; Paul Boehm, Ingo Claßen, Christian Dimitrovici, Gottfried Eggers, Andreas Fett, Werner Fey, Martin Große-Rhode, Horst Hansen, Michael Löwe, Catharina Riekhoff, Wolfram Schulte, Dietmar Wolz

Technische Universität Braunschweig: *Hans-Dieter Ehrich*; Martin Gogolla

Universität Bremen: *Bernd Krieg-Brückner (Coordinator), Hans-Jörg Kreowski*; Berthold Hoffmann, Stefan Kahrs, Junbo Liu, Detlef Plump, Zhenyu Qian

Universität Dortmund: *Harald Ganzinger*; Hubert Bertling, Michael Hanus, Renate Schäfers

University of Edinburgh: *Rod Burstall, Don Sannella*; Jordi Farrès-Casals, Edmund Kazmierczak, Luo Zhaohui

Università di Genova: *Egidio Astesiano*; Maura Cerioli, Alessandro Giovini, Gianna Reggio, Elena Zucca

Technische Universität München: *Manfred Broy*; Michael Breu, Frank Dederichs, Heinrich Hußmann, Rainer Weber

Centre de Recherche en Informatique de Nancy: *Pierre Lescanne, Jean-Luc Rémy, Hélène Kirchner*; Wadoud Bousdira, Isabelle Gnaedig, Mikulas Hermann, Claude Kirchner, Denis Lugiez, Aristide Megrelis, Michaël Rusinowitch

Katholieke Universiteit Nijmegen: *Helmut Partsch*; N.W.P. van Diepen

Université de Paris-Sud, Orsay: *Marie-Claude Gaudel, Jean-Pierre Jouannaud*; Michel Bidoit, Gilles Bernot, Anne Blanchard, Alexandre Boudet, Christine Choppy, Evelyne Contejean, Pierre Dauchy, Hervé Devie, Marta Franova, Martin Gaschignard, Thierry Heuillard, Pascale Le Gall, Bruno Marre, Thierry Moineau, Pan Quing-Bin, Frédéric Voisin

Universität Passau: *Martin Wirsing*; Ruth Breu, Michael Gengenbach, Alfons Geser, Thomas Grünler, Rolf Hennicker, Friederike Nickl, Peter Padawitz, Thomas Streicher

Scientific Correspondents: Jan Bergstra, Amsterdam; Didier Bert, Grenoble; Bruno Courcelle, Bordeaux; Ole-Johan Dahl, Oslo; Joseph Goguen, Oxford; Friedrich W. von Henke, Ulm; Klaus P. Jantke, Leipzig; Franz Lichtenberger, Linz; Jacques Loeckx, Saarbrücken; Tom Maibaum, London; Bernhard Möller, München; Ugo Montanari, Pisa; Peter Mosses, Aarhus; Tobias Nipkow, Cambridge; Olaf Owe, Oslo; Ernst-Rüdiger Olderog, Oldenburg; Francesco Parisi-Presicce, L'Aquila; Axel Poigné, St. Augustin; Horst Reichel, Dresden; Amilcar Sernadas, Lisbon; Gerd Smolka, Stuttgart; Andrzej Tarlecki, Warsaw; Muffy Thomas, Glasgow

Contents

Introduction   **1**

1 Basic Foundations   **7**
   1.1 Basic Semantic Constructions and Constraints   7
   1.2 Structure and Refinement   8
      1.2.1 Structuring Operators   9
      1.2.2 Parameterized Specifications and Module Specifications 10
      1.2.3 Vertical Development and Implementation Relations 12
   1.3 Expressive Power of Specification Approaches   13

2 Models and Logics   **15**
   2.1 Partiality and Non-Strictness   15
   2.2 Order-Sortedness and Polymorphism   16
   2.3 Higher-Order Functions and Infinite Objects   18
   2.4 Non-Determinism and Concurrency   19
   2.5 Institutions   22

3 Development Concepts   **25**
   3.1 Requirements Engineering   25
   3.2 Transformation of Specifications   26
   3.3 Reusability   29
   3.4 Exception Handling   30
   3.5 Specification Languages   31

4 Support Tools   **35**
   4.1 Specification Environments and Development Systems   35
   4.2 Executable Specifications and Prototyping   37
      4.2.1 Techniques Based on Rewriting   37
      4.2.2 Graph Reduction   37
   4.3 Theorem Proving   38
      4.3.1 First-Order Logic   38
      4.3.2 First-Order Logic with Equality   39
      4.3.3 Higher-Order Logic   39
      4.3.4 Computer-Aided Proof Checking   39
   4.4 Term Rewriting   41
      4.4.1 Notions of Term Rewriting   41
      4.4.2 Unification and Matching   42

      4.4.3   Termination of Rewrite Systems 44

      4.4.4   Completion 45

5 Applications   **49**

  5.1 Software Development Process 49

      5.1.1   Formalization of the Development Process 50

      5.1.2   Applications Within the Development Process 50

      5.1.3   Software Modularity 51

  5.2 Programming Languages 52

      5.2.1   Semantics of Programming Languages 52

      5.2.2   Functional Programming 53

      5.2.3   Logic Programming 54

      5.2.4   Object-Oriented Programming 54

  5.3 Databases and Knowledge Bases 56

Bibliography   **59**

Introduction

A great deal of work has been devoted to methods of specification based on the simple idea that a functional program can be modelled as a *many-sorted algebra*, i.e. as a number of sets of data values (one set of values for each data type) together with a number of total functions on those sets corresponding to the functions in the program. This abstracts away from the algorithms used to compute the functions and how those algorithms are expressed in a given programming language, focusing instead on the representation of data and the input/output behaviour of functions. The pioneering work in this area is [Zil 74], [Gut 75], [GTW 76], of which the latter — the so-called *initial algebra approach* — is the most formal. This idea was soon taken up by other workers, see e.g. [GGM 76], [GHM 76], [BG 77], [GHM 78]. Today the field of algebraic specification has grown into one of the major areas of research in theoretical computer science. More than fifteen years of research have led to an abundance of competing and complementary theories and approaches. The algebraic approach provides a conceptual basis, theoretical foundations and prototype tools for the stepwise formal development of correct system components from their specifications, and thus covers the whole software development process from the specification of requirements to the finished system. These methods are potentially applicable to the development of correct hardware systems as well.

Technological Perspectives

System Specification and Development

In software technology, methods and development environments for the construction of software components are becoming increasingly important. The decomposition of systems into self-contained components supports a breakdown of the production process in a "software factory". Generic reusable components avoid duplication of development effort, ease prototyping and speed up system construction.

An industry of interchangeable and widely-marketable software components is only possible if the functionality of components can be precisely specified. It is highly desirable to specify the properties of a component which are required for correctness without mentioning additional properties which some particular implementation of the component happens to possess. Such a requirement specification must be precise and unambiguous but as loose as possible to avoid over-specification, leaving freedom for different design decisions by the implementor. This leads ultimately to decreased cost and increased efficiency of the software development process. The particular design implementing this specification should remain hidden to ease replacement of components at the development stage, for example of a prototype component by a final implementation, and during system evolution when requirements change and updates are required. In an industry of software components, hiding the details of the design of a component might also be desirable for proprietary reasons.

The state of the art in software technology allows the specification of the syntactic aspects of a software component only, that is of the (data) types and operations it provides. The user and implementor of a software component usually have to rely on natural language comments for information about the semantics of these types and operations. This poses a severe danger of misinterpretation, inconsistency and incompleteness because of the inherent lack of precision of natural language. There is no way to increase confidence by any means of verification other than inspection of the code of the implementation. This violation of the information-hiding principle makes exchanging the implementation of isolated components in the process of system improvement and evolution extremely cumbersome if not impossible.

The algebraic approach supports the precise specification of the semantic aspects of component interfaces. It allows loose, property-oriented requirement specifications that characterise a class of acceptable models (implementations). It also allows the separate, hidden specification of a particular design. Perhaps most importantly, the implementation relation between a requirement specification and a design specification, that is the correctness of the design with respect to the requirement specification, can be formally verified. The stepwise development of improved, more detailed versions of components can be supported by automated tools, including the verification of correctness for each step. The development process itself can be formalised, and generic software development methods and associated interactive tools exist in prototype versions.

Alternative formal approaches which use a purely model-oriented approach, i.e. specifying the meaning of a component by giving a very abstract implementation (for example by sets and sequences in a functional programming language) may give away more detail about the particular design than desirable since they specify a particular model. The transition to a different design may be very difficult since a specification of the abstract properties common to both is not available.

Emerging Impact on Software Technology

Algebraic techniques have already played a dominant role in several national and international research projects. The CIP project in Munich has shown how algebraic specification techniques can be used in a large-scale research project for program transformation and software development. In the ACT project in Berlin it was shown how the idea of generic software design using parameterized specifications and modularization can be combined with the concept of compositionality known from denotational semantics. In the specification language PLUSS developed in Paris, linguistic support is proposed for the specification development process. Many theoretical foundations of algebraic specifications and practical aspects of formal software development are addressed in the languages CLEAR and Extended ML that were designed in Edinburgh. Algebraic specification techniques have been used in various ESPRIT projects such as DRAGON, FOR-ME-TOO, GRASPIN, METEOR, PEACOCK, PROSPECTRA, RAISE and SEDOS, and these techniques will be used in ESPRIT II projects as well. The formal definition of Ada under the EC Multi-Annual Programme used algebraic specification techniques. Projects in the USA include the development of the OBJ executable specification language at SRI International, and the development of the LARCH specification language at MIT and DEC Systems Research Center. In all these projects, research institutions and industry are cooperating to produce software development methods and tools based on algebraic techniques.

At the moment, only prototype tools exist and there is a lack of knowledge about algebraic techniques in industry. The long-term tendency is towards the use of such techniques and of the corresponding tools and environments in industrial software development. There are strong efforts underway at various universities to teach algebraic methods in theoretical and practical courses and to integrate them into Computer Science curricula at the undergraduate and postgraduate level.

Interaction between Theory and Applications

Early developments in the field of algebraic specifications were aimed at achieving an adequate understanding of concepts like "specification" and "refinement". This work used known techniques from universal algebra, logic and category theory and were effectively limited in relevance to the specification and development of simply-typed first-order terminating functional programs without side-effects or exceptions. But soon a number of extensions took place, driven by the need to handle practical problems. On one hand, various different logical systems were introduced to cope with more complex features of programs. On the other hand, structuring techniques, including parameterization and modularization concepts, were developed in order to cope with large-scale specifications.

These developments of the theory were driven by the need to handle an extended range of applications. Algebraic techniques are not only used for the specification of abstract data types but also for the specification of complete software systems, for the formal description of the program development process, for the uniform definition of the syntax and semantics of programming languages, for data bases and information systems, and so forth. Currently we observe the advance of new programming paradigms such as object-oriented, logic and higher-order functional programming, and further application areas such as the description of hardware structures, and concurrent distributed systems. First approaches to the extension of algebraic approaches to accommodate these new application areas are already visible. However, it will be a major task to generalise the foundations of algebraic methods in a comprehensive way so that they fully meet the requirements of these new applications.

It is important that algebraic approaches benefit from results obtained in other areas of Computer Science. It has to be studied to what degree, for instance, principles of expert systems can be utilised for the development of algebraic specifications, or how elements from present programming environments (such as version control and configuration management) can be used as tools in algebraic approaches. An obvious connection exists with the area of theorem proving since computer support for verification is the kernel of any serious algebraic specification or development environment. There are connections with other issues as well, e.g. with graphic environments, with data base techniques, concurrency, communication, and other distributed system techniques.

4

This Book

This book is an annotated bibliography which attempts to provide an up-to-date overview of most past and present work on algebraic specification for researchers in algebraic specification and neighbouring fields. A review of the main topics of current and past research is given, with some indication of how the different approaches are related and pointers to relevant papers. Sometimes "topics to be investigated" are indicated, listing some of the gaps in the current state of knowledge.

The term "algebraic specification" has been used by different people at different times to refer to different things. Originally it referred to the use of (many-sorted) algebras to model programs, and the use of equational axioms to write specifications. This was sufficient to handle simple specifications of total first-order functions, but not much more. Nowadays, more complicated notions of algebra are used to take account of partial functions, higher-order functions, etc., and more sophisticated logical systems are used to write axioms describing such algebras (see Chapter 2). Although the use of the label "algebraic" no longer seems appropriate in this context, it is still widely used. Probably the feature which unifies all approaches under this banner is the use of algebra-like models of some kind in order to concentrate on the functional behaviour of software systems and the representation of data. Specifications describe such models via the use of axioms in some logical system which normally includes equality as a primitive.

No attempt is made here to provide an introduction to algebraic specifications. For such an introduction, the reader is referred to any one of the textbooks and monographs which have appeared during the past few years. In order of publication, these include [Kla 83], [EM 85], [Rei 87], [Pad 88], [EGL 89], [HL 89], [EM 90] and [Par 90]. Several collections of papers on the topic have been published, including [Kre 85b], [ST 88b], [WB 89c] and [BHK 89]. A previous annotated bibliography of papers on algebraic specification is [KL 83].

The field of algebraic specification is divided here into five main topics. Any such division is difficult; there is inevitably significant overlap between parts.

Chapter 1: Basic Foundations

A discussion which arose early in the history of work on algebraic specifications concerned the choice of semantics of a specification. In the context of purely equational (or conditional equational) specifications, the obvious choice of taking the class of all algebras which are models of the axioms is ruled out since this will always admit undesirable trivial models. An early suggestion was to restrict attention to the *initial* object(s) in this category of models; another possibility is to restrict attention to the *terminal* object(s) in a certain sub-category of models; other choices are also possible (Section 1.1). As soon as non-trivial examples are considered, it becomes obvious that large specifications are unmanageable unless they are built in a structured fashion from smaller specifications using *specification-building operations* of various kinds (Section 1.2.1) and mechanisms for *parameterization* and *modularization* of specifications (Section 1.2.2). The decision to structure specifications also makes it necessary to modify the choice of semantics by introducing *constraints* which take account of the hierarchical way in which specifications are put together (Section 1.1). The interest in specifications stem largely from their intended role in the formal program development process whereby programs are evolved from specifications by means of successive refinement or *implementation* steps. An important question is thus the definition of the implementation relation (Section 1.2.3); this is another area in which there is no single obviously correct choice. With many different choices of specification approach (initial/final models, with/without parameterization, with/without constraints, etc.) the question of the relative expressive power of the different approaches arises (Section 1.3).

Chapter 2: Models and Logics

Any approach to algebraic specification must be based on some notion of algebra and some choice of logical system in which to write axioms. Early approaches were based on many-sorted algebras and equational axioms. Soon it became clear that this is not always flexible enough. Some data types and functions can only be described in an awkward fashion using equational logic, and there are some cases where equations are not powerful enough. Conditional equations or predicates give more power but still not enough for some purposes. It is even more apparent that more complicated logical systems and more complicated notions of algebra are needed to cope with "awkward" aspects of programs such as: non-terminating, partial and non-strict functions (Section 2.1); coercions/subtypes, overloaded functions and polymorphic types (Section 2.2); higher-order functions and infinite objects (Section 2.3); non-deterministic functions and concurrent systems (Section 2.4). A great deal of work has been devoted to enriching the basic algebraic specification framework to deal with these complications; a related area is the specification of functions which may produce errors (Section 3.4). It turns out that much of the work on algebraic specifications that has been done is actually independent of the notion of algebra and the logic used to write axioms: it is possible to formulate many results in the context of an arbitrary *institution* (Section 2.5).

Chapter 3: Development Concepts

Work on algebraic specifications aims to provide conceptual and methodological support for all aspects of the software development process. An early phase of the software life-cycle is the construction of the requirement specification, which lists the properties which the desired system is to satisfy. An important problem is how to translate the often vague wishes of the customer into a formal requirement specification: this is the topic of *requirements engineering* (Section 3.1). Once a specification is available, various methods are available for *transforming* it into an equivalent specification or into an executable program which is correct by construction (Section 3.2). There are relations between these methods and program synthesis and the "proofs as programs" paradigm. One of the advantages of formally developing programs from specifications is the possibility for correct *reuse* of previously-developed program components based on their specifications (Section 3.3). A well-known problem in software development is the importance and difficulty of specifying the error-handling characteristics of a software system. Various methods for specifying functions which may produce errors have been developed within the algebraic approach (Section 3.4); all of these involve some fundamental change to the notion of algebra and the logical system used to write axioms (cf. Chapter 2). Practical use of algebraic specifications in program development requires convenient notations for writing specifications, i.e. *specification languages* (Section 3.5). Many such languages have been developed, providing different combinations of the features discussed in Chapters 1 and 2.

Chapter 4: Support Tools

The use of algebraic specifications in practical software development demands a range of machine-based tools to support various software development activities. A number of integrated specification *support systems* have been produced, aiding the construction of specifications and checking of their properties, and covering certain aspects of the development of programs from specifications (Section 4.1). When specifications include equational or conditional equational axioms only, it is possible under certain conditions to use them directly as high-level *prototypes*, running test cases in order to check that the specification describes what is intended (Section 4.2). An obviously important activity in connection with formal specifications of any kind is *proving theorems* in the context of a specification (Section 4.3). One problem here is coping with the variety of logical systems discussed in Chapter 2. If equational axioms or conditional equational axioms are adequate for the needs at hand, then *term rewriting* provides techniques for fast theorem proving (Section 4.4). This is an extensively-developed research area; important sub-topics concern the special problems of *conditional term rewriting* (Section 4.4.1), unification, matching and *narrowing* (Section 4.4.2), *proofs of termination* of rewrite systems using sophisticated orderings on the set of terms (Section 4.4.3), and Knuth-Bendix-style *completion* of term rewriting systems (Section 4.4.4). Term rewriting techniques are useful for program transformation, symbolic simplification, etc. as well as for theorem proving.

Chapter 5: Applications

There are extensive areas of application of work on algebraic specifications in other areas of Computer Science. Some important applications and connections with other areas are dealt with in earlier chapters (e.g. the specification of concurrent systems is discussed in Section 2.4, and theorem proving is discussed in Section 4.3). A few other such applications are covered here. The first concerns the use of methods of algebraic specification to specify and reason about the program development process itself (Section 5.1) and the use of algebraic techniques in the phases involved in this process. Sub-topics include strategies for testing programs based on their specifications (Section 5.1.2) and software modularity (Section 5.1.3; cf. Section 1.2.2). Algebraic specification methods can be used to specify the semantics of programming languages (Section 5.2.1), provided that algebras are used which are capable of successfully modelling the features present in the programming language at hand (non-termination, concurrency, etc. — see Chapter 2). There are relationships between work on algebraic specification and work on functional programming languages (Section 5.2.2; cf. executable specifications, Section 4.2, and term rewriting, Section 4.4), logic programming languages (Section 5.2.3), and object-oriented programming languages (Section 5.2.4). Algebraic specifications have also been applied in the area of databases and knowledge bases (Section 5.3).

Chapter 1

Basic Foundations

1.1 Basic Semantic Constructions and Constraints

When defining the semantics of a specification we have, in principle, two choices: considering the whole class of models satisfying the specification (this is usually called *loose* semantics) or restricting the semantics to a certain subclass of "interesting" models. Then the question is to decide what the concept of "interesting" should be. The choice between one option or the other depends on the power of the specification language used. If the language is not powerful enough, then among all the models satisfying a given specification there will probably be many non-interesting or degenerate ones that, because of the lack of power of the language, cannot be ruled out (for instance, this is the case when using pure equational logic). Loose semantics is appropriate for specification and program development [BW 82b], [BP 83], [ST 89], [OSC 89], whereas more restrictive semantics may be interesting for final design specifications.

Apart from loose semantics, the main approaches have been the following:

1. *Initial* semantics [GTW 76] (for an overview see [EM 85]): The interesting models are considered to be the initial objects in the category of all models. An initial algebra for an equational specification SP is characterized by the fact that it satisfies only those equations which hold in all models of SP; thus initial algebra semantics is closely related to rewriting (see Section 4.4) and therefore well-suited for rapid prototyping of specifications.

2. *Final* semantics [GGM 76, Wan 79]: In this case the interesting models are considered to be the terminal objects of a certain sub-category of the category of all the models. Final algebra semantics represents the "mathematical" semantics of a specification by which the identity of a data value is determined by its behaviour in all contexts.

3. *Term-generated algebra* semantics [BW 82b] (for an overview, see [Wir 90]): The semantics of a specification is considered to be all algebras satisfying the specification and containing no "junk", i.e. every value in the algebra is the result of evaluating a ground term. Initial and final algebras are special "extremal" models of this semantics [BDPPW 79], [BPW 84].

At present, some other semantic constructions have been proposed for defining the meaning of specifications. Specifically, with some tradition now, is the so-called *behavioural* semantics [Rei 81], [GM 82], [ST 87a], [Sch 87b], [Hen 88], [NO 88], [ONE 89] and the recent proposal of *ultra-loose* semantics [WB 89b]. Moreover, new semantic paradigms have been devised in order to provide sensible semantics for algebraic specifications of processes [AW 89], [AGR 88a].

These semantic constructions are based, not on restricting the class of models, but on giving a different interpretation to the satisfaction relation. Then, at least for the behavioural case, the class of models may be restricted along the ideas outlined above [NO 88], or not restricted. The main idea in behaviour semantics is that (given some notion of observation) it is not so important whether a model satisfies a given formula or not, but rather whether it satisfies all its observable consequences. The main idea of ultra-loose semantics is that all possible implementations should be considered as models of a specification.

In some approaches, restrictions to the class of models of a given specification are given explicitly using so-called *constraints*. A constraint is a semantic construction "fixing" or "restricting" the interpretation of a specification contained within a larger one. As a consequence, the semantics of this larger specification is also restricted accordingly.

Constraints were first defined and used by Reichel [Rei 80] for giving semantics to *canons*. In his approach, a constraint designates a part of a specification that is to be interpreted initially (or to be more accurate, freely). This kind of constraint has been called a *data* or *free generating* constraint. They were the basis of the semantic definition of CLEAR [BG 80] and of other specification languages [ETLZ 84].

In [SW 82], Sannella and Wirsing proposed a different kind of constraint, called *hierarchy* constraints, related to loose semantics in the same way as data constraints are related to initial semantics. Similar constraints are also introduced in the PLUSS specification language [Bid 89].

Wagner and Ehrig in [WE 87] defined a language for the definition of constraints and showed that any constraint in this language may be expressed in a canonical form in terms of three basic operations for constraint definition: *generation, translation* and *reflection*.

In [CO 88], constraints are used to work with incomplete specifications and a new inheritance relation between such specifications is defined to express the concept of "adding detail". It is shown that parameterization is not needed when dealing with this kind of relation. However, some work has to be done concerning the foundations of this approach. In particular, results have to be obtained which characterize the correctness conditions under which the constructions work "properly".

1.2   Structure and Refinement

In the earliest work on algebraic specification, abstract data types were specified by a *theory*, i.e. a signature together with a set of axioms. For small specifications such an approach is adequate, but it is more convenient to build large and complex specifications in a structured way by putting together small specifications. Structuring large specifications into smaller component specifications that can be treated separately facilitates their construction, understanding, analysis and implementation, and enhances reusability.

These ideas have been incorporated in virtually all algebraic specification languages since CLEAR [BG 77]. Concepts which were developed to support structured specifications include *constraints* (Section 1.1), a wide range of different *specification-building operations*

(Section 1.2.1), and various different approaches to *parameterization* and *modularization* (Section 1.2.2).

Together with the need to build large specifications from smaller ones by appropriate combinations, there is the need to impose a hierarchical organization that reflects the structure of specifications and of the design process by which they have been created. A good hierarchical organization not only enhances understandability of specifications but may also simplify their construction making possible the reuse of portions of previously existing specifications.

The most classical approach consists in basing hierarchical organization on the concept of *enrichment* or *extension* [WPPDB 83]. However, at the present time, the most accepted approach is based on the notion of two-dimensional specification design [GB 80]. The horizontal structure of such a hierarchical organization corresponds to enrichments or extensions and the vertical structure to specification refinement (see Section 1.2.3).

1.2.1 Structuring Operators

The need to build large specifications by combining or extending smaller ones in a structured manner was recognized very early on. In [GH 78], specifications were built by successive extension of previously existing ones; moreover, the notions of *hierarchical consistency* and *sufficient completeness*, as the conditions to be achieved by extensions in order for them to be considered correct, were defined (see also [Ber 87]).

Nowadays, algebraic specification languages (e.g. CLEAR [BG 80], ACT ONE [EFH 83a], ACT TWO [Fey 88], ASL [SW 83], OBJ3 [GW 88], Extended ML [ST 85], CIP-L [CIP 85], PLUSS [Gau 85], LARCH [GH 86c], OBSCURE [LL 88], PA^{mn}dA-S [Kri 90c]) offer a full range of operators for building specifications. Among these, there are various enrichment primitives that reflect various combinations of hierarchical conditions such as sufficient completeness and hierarchical consistency (e.g. the enrichment primitives *using*, *extending* and *protecting* in OBJ3, or the enrichment primitives *assumes*, *imports* and *includes* in LARCH). In the PLUSS specification language, completed specification components and specifications under development are distinguished not only at the level of the enrichment specification-building primitives but also by a (syntactic) distinction between the specification modules themselves. Thus, appropriate syntactic rules prevent enriching completed specification components using overly permissive enrichment primitives, while this is allowed for specifications under development.

Other specification building operations that may be commonly found in all specification languages are *union* and *actualization*. Union or combination is the operation of putting together two or more specifications (which possibly have common sub-specifications). Actualization is the operation of instantiating a parameterized specification. In most languages, parameterized specifications must explicitly declare their formal parameters. However, in some others, for instance LOOK [ETLZ 84] and GSBL [CO 88], [Clé 89], actualization may be performed by matching any sub-component of a specification with a given actual parameter. This, obviously, provides additional flexibility.

Another essential kind of operation which may be found in all specification languages is *renaming*. This is used to avoid name conflicts and to increase readability of specifications.

Also, specification languages provide different forms of abstraction operators, such as *derive*, *restrict* or *behaviour* which allow sorts or operations to be forgotten, unreachable values to be eliminated or which perform behavioural abstraction.

Finally, it must be considered that in the design of specification languages, as in the design of programming languages, there is a fundamental tension between the desire for simplicity and the need for convenience. Some specification languages (e.g. the so-called "kernel" specification language ASL) tend toward the former extreme, with a small number of very powerful structuring operators which are not at all convenient to use. Most other specification languages tend toward the latter extreme, with structuring operators which automatically take care of name conflicts at the cost of a rather complex semantics. The structuring operators in the more complex user-friendly specification languages may be defined in terms of those in a simpler language; e.g. the semantics of Extended ML and PLUSS are given by translation into ASL.

Topics to be Investigated

Even though the co-existence of various enrichment specification-building primitives in a specification language may stem from methodological considerations, it is still the case that the mathematical foundations of these structuring concepts should be more deeply investigated. More precisely, the interactions between the choice of the underlying semantical framework (initial, final, loose, etc.), the specification-building primitives and modularity or reusability raises difficult problems. Therefore, more sophisticated structuring concepts (such as e.g. those developed in [Bid 88]) should be investigated.

1.2.2   Parameterized Specifications and Module Specifications

Parameterized data types and generic program modules have been an important step forward on the way to more powerful abstract constructs for software design.

Parameterized specifications were introduced in [BG 77], [TWW 78], [BG 80], [Ehr 82]. In [TWW 78] the semantics of a parameterized specification was defined in terms of free functors, while in [BG 77], [BG 80], [Ehr 82], working at the specification level, parameter passing was defined in terms of pushouts (a set-theoretic version of this is given in [San 84]). In [EKTWW 84] the two approaches were combined. In this framework, correctness of parameterized specifications was defined in terms of the properties of *actual parameter protection* and *passing compatibility*, which were proved equivalent to persistency of the associated free functor [EKTWW 84], [Ore 87a]. In [Ehr 81] this framework is extended to deal with parameterized specifications with requirements, and [NO 87b], [Pad 84], [Pad 85] generalize the basic results to deal with parameterized specifications with boolean constraints.

Ganzinger [Gan 83], defined parameterized specifications within the tradition of final semantics and also provided a characterization of persistency in terms of hierarchy consistency and sufficient completeness properties. Similar results have been obtained by several authors for different approaches to parameterized specifications with behavioural semantics [GM 82], [Rei 81], [Rei 85], [Niv 87], [NO 88] and with term generated semantics [WB 82].

A completely different approach is taken in ASL [SW 83], in which parameterized specifications are presented as computable transformations on specifications, in the style of λ-calculus.

Module specifications may be seen as a generalization of parameterized specifications. Several approaches with different aims have been developed.

In [BEP 87], [EW 85], [EFP 86], [WE 86] a module concept is defined to serve as a basis for modular specification development. According to this approach, a module specification consists of a realization specification, a formal parameter specification and explicit import and export interfaces. The theory of module specifications combining initial and loose semantics [Ehr 84] and their interconnections (horizontal structuring) is well-developed in the basic algebraic case with persistent (as well as conservative) free functors. The basic horizontal structuring operations for such module specifications are "renaming", "union" and "actualization". Others are "extension" [BEP 87], "recursion" [Par 87], "product" and "iteration" [Par 88]. There are first ideas how to extend these concepts to algebraic specifications with constraints [EW 86], [EFPB 86] and how to handle the development of specifications (vertical development) [EFHLP 87], [EM 90]. This concept of module is the basis of the specification language ACT TWO [Fey 86], [Fey 88].

The module system of the Standard ML programming language [HMM 86] is adopted by the Extended ML specification language [ST 85], [ST 86], [ST 89]. Its aims are to serve as the basis for the modular development of (ML) programs from specifications. The module system of Standard ML includes facilities designed to allow large programs to be structured into self-contained program units with explicitly-specified interfaces. In this system, interfaces (signatures) and their implementations (structures) are defined separately. Structures may be built on top of existing structures, so each one is actually a hierarchy of structures. Functors are "parameterized" structures; the application of a functor to a structure yields a structure. A functor has both an input signature describing structures to which it may be applied, and an output signature describing the result of an application. The development of programs from specifications is simplified by the fact that the mechanisms used for structuring specifications and programs are identical.

A related modules system is Pebble [BL 88], which abandons the distinction between type and value. This gives more power and simplifies matters but as a consequence it sacrifices guaranteed termination for typechecking.

Topics to be Investigated

Modules systems need consolidation. The theory should be extended in order to study module and configuration families for version handling [EFHJL 89], [EFHLJLP 89], [EFHLJ 89], to study the use of modules within distributed systems [WE 88], and to integrate the concepts into a specification language for modular systems. Also, a thorny issue in the design of modules systems is the manner in which sharing of common sub-components is specified and controlled. Recent investigations suggest that there is a way of simplifying and generalising the treatment of sharing using dependent types. With respect to the modules system developed by the Berlin group, module specifications with constraints, vertical development, and compatibility of horizontal structuring with vertical development have to be studied in more detail. Moreover this should be compared and combined with different notions of observational and behavioural abstraction. Finally, for practical applications it might be useful to relax the rather strong conditions concerning persistency such that the main results concerning correctness and compositionality remain valid [HL 88].

1.2.3 Vertical Development and Implementation Relations

Formal specifications are the basis for the use of formal methods in software development. According to this approach, programs may be seen as the result of a refinement process starting from a high-level specification and ending with a low-level program. If each refinement step can be proven correct, then the resulting program is guaranteed to satisfy the original specification.

In order to make this process precise, an adequate formal notion of refinement step is required. During the past ten years there has been a great deal of work on this topic; more than twenty different definitions have been advocated in the literature. Summarising, we may consider that a specification SP1 may refine vertically another specification SP2 in three different ways:

1. The class of models of SP1 is, in some sense, contained in the class of models of SP2. This means that, in going from SP2 to SP1, some design decisions have been taken, so that the options for the final "implementation" have been constrained. This notion has been developed by [SW 83], [ST 87a], [Sch 87b]. Also, the subclass relation that may be found in [CO 88], [OSC 89] may be seen as a special case of such refinements.

2. The language of SP1 is "less abstract" than the language of SP2. For instance, in [BW 88a] the relation between explicit and implicit definition in algebraic specification is studied. Also, in [Ore 85] and in [KS 88] this is done for equational specifications and recursive definitions.

3. SP2 may be seen as "simulating" SP1. This is the classical notion of implementation that goes back to the pioneering paper of Hoare [Hoa 72]. This notion has been developed by [GTW 76], [GHM 76], [EKP 78], [EKP 79], [Ehr 82], [EKMP 82], [GM 82], [SW 82], [EK 83], [Gan 83], [BBC 86b], [BMPW 86] and [Sch 87b] among others. Probably the most influential of these is [EKMP 82].

A recent approach which unifies and generalizes all previous approaches is [ST 87b]. This definition clarifies the role of certain properties (both vertical and horizontal composability [GB 80]) which many notions lack [Ore 83], [Ore 84], [Ore 86]. *Vertical* composability is essential for stepwise program development since it allows successive correct refinements to be composed into a single correct refinement step. *Horizontal* composability is necessary for modular program development since it allows correct refinements of separate modules of a program to be combined into a single correct refinement of the whole program. This notion of refinement works in the context of an arbitrary institution (see Section 2.5) and it is even possible to change institutions in the course of a refinement step (so for example refining an equational specification to yield a Hoare-logic specification of an imperative program).

These notions of implementation may be extended to deal with module specifications. For instance, module refinements in Extended ML are studied in [ST 89]. In [Sch 87b], a language-independent theory of module refinements and implementations is given that allows the horizontal and vertical composition of implementation steps. Also the theory of algebraic module specifications [BEP 87] with horizontal structuring operations is extended in [EFHLP 87], [EM 90] by vertical development steps leading from abstract module specifications to more concrete versions. The basic concept of refinement is given by specification morphisms between corresponding parameter, export and import interface specifications. It is shown that refinement is compatible with the horizontal structuring operations composition, actualization and union. This allows modular vertical development. Other kinds of vertical steps between module specifications are *simulation* and *transformation*.

Topics to be Investigated

The definition of refinement in [ST 87b] is model-based rather than syntax-based. In order to use this notion in formal program development it is necessary to have some straightforward way of proving refinement steps correct. The limited experience so far obtained with such proofs suggests that they tend to follow a certain pattern, centered around a proof by induction over terms of a certain form. This leads us to believe that it should be possible to develop methods for proving refinement steps correct which would allow the majority of cases to be handled more or less routinely. Once this is done, it will be possible to implement a refinement step verifier with the help of a theorem prover. As with verification condition generators which automatically invent appropriate invariant assertions for each loop in an imperative program, the idea would be to automatically generate from a given refinement step a theorem to be proved which if true would guarantee the correctness of that step. The methods developed in [Sch 90] for reasoning about behaviourally equivalent algebras using so-called correspondences should come in useful here. Some syntax-oriented methods which seem more attractive for mechanized proofs of correctness are [Hen 88], [Hen 89] and [Far 89].

1.3 Expressive Power of Specification Approaches

In order to understand the expressive power and the limitations of the different specification methods it is interesting to analyse their computability aspects. The main clarifications are due to Bergstra and Tucker who undertook a systematic study of the computability of abstract data types in a rich series of papers (see e.g. [BT 83]; for an overview see [MG 85] or [BT 87]).

An early question was the *hidden function* problem [Maj 79], [TWW 78]; Bergstra and Tucker proved that (finite equational) specifications without hidden functions are not expressive enough to specify all recursive data structures [BT 87]. On the other hand, they showed that initial algebra specifications with hidden functions describe exactly all semicomputable algebras whereas conditional equational terminal algebra specifications with hidden functions describe exactly all co-semicomputable algebras [BT 83]. A still open question is whether the latter result also holds for specifications with purely equational axioms.

The computability of parameterized abstract data types is studied by Bergstra and Klop [BK 81]. In [BBTW 81] characterization theorems for hierarchical specifications and partial algebra specifications are given, where it is shown that the use of constraints in full generality increases the power of specifications so much that models of algebraic theories defined by constrained specifications may lie outside the arithmetic hierarchy. Partial algebra specifications are also analysed by Kaphengst [Kap 81]. First results on the expressive power of specification-building operations can be found in [Wir 86]. The computational complexity of abstract data types is studied in [LB 81], [EM 81], [AT 82].

Researchers have introduced various syntactic features (such as polymorphism, exception handling, definedness predicates, Horn clauses, ordered sorts, based specifications etc.), generalising and supplementing the traditional concepts of equational specifications. On the semantical level, a variety of different data type constructions (such as the initial algebra construction, image factorization, restriction, forgetting, deriving, etc.) correspond to such specification techniques. The expressive power of these techniques — in particular when they are combined with each other — has not yet been studied systematically.

Topics to be Investigated

What are the limits of the expressive power of specification techniques? Which techniques can be combined with which others? How do combinations of techniques effect their expressive power? How can the expressive power of the techniques be compared with each other? The answers will improve insight into the usefulness of algebraic specifications and will direct the design of future algebraic specification languages, or justify the existing ones.

Chapter 2

Models and Logics

2.1 Partiality and Non-Strictness

Nowadays it seems quite clear that if algebraic specifications are to be used as a powerful and realistic tool for the development of complex systems they should permit the specification of partial functions. This gives a lot of flexibility and is natural since in computer science one has to deal with the fact that certain algorithms and recursive functions do not always terminate. As soon as partial functions are incorporated there is also the question of whether non-strict functions should be incorporated, too. If algebraic specifications are to accommodate styles of functional programming and constructs dealing with infinite objects, the incorporation of so-called "non-strict" functions including non-strict constructor functions is necessary.

Algebraic specifications with partial functions have been investigated for many years. The Munich CIP Group [BW 82b] investigated from the very beginning of the idea of algebraic data types the possibility of working with algebraic specifications that specify partial algebras [BW 82a]. Further work has been done on giving an algebraic theory based on the concept of partial algebras for specifying the semantics of programming languages [Pep 79], [BPPW 80], [BPW 80], [BW 80], [BPW 87], [WPPDB 83], [BPW 84]. Also, partiality has been dealt with by means of order-sortedness [GM 83], [SNGM 89] (see Section 2.2), error specifications (see Section 3.4) and based specification [Kre 87]. The books [Bur 86] and [Rei 87] lay a solid foundation for the mathematical treatment of partial algebras.

There are essentially two ways of specifying partial functions. One way is to explicitly give the domain of definition of each function (for example, by means of a definedness predicate [BW 82a] or as the set of solutions of a system of equations [Rei 87]). The other way is to model partial algebras using total algebras where each carrier set is partitioned into a set of acceptable values and a set of unacceptable ones (the latter set sometimes contains a single element representing "undefined"). A function is considered to be defined for a given argument if it delivers an acceptable value for that argument. Partiality introduced by means of error specifications is of this second type. In this case, special rules have to be given to deal with the application of functions to the undefined element (resp. the unacceptable elements). If one assumes that all functions are *strict*, which means they produce undefined whenever one of the arguments is undefined, one stays in the classical framework of partial functions and just uses a total representation of partial functions. If, however, one decides to allow functions to produce a well-defined result even when some argument is undefined, then we speak of *non-strict* functions [BW 83c]. Non-strict functions are important in the framework of infinite objects and special constructs in functional programming such as if-then-else. In many cases additional requirements are assumed for non-strict functions such as *monotonicity*, *continuity* or *regularity*.

Topics to be Investigated

The way in which partial functions are to be incorporated into the algebraic specification framework needs consolidation. Unification of the various approaches seems to be needed especially in the light of the requirement that non-strict functions should also be treated within this framework. The implications of the treatment of partial functions on the deductive theory should be examined. A special question is the meaning of equality in the presence of partial functions and its consequences with respect to the deductive theory. Some results have been obtained recently in this direction [AC 89]. Also the relationship to term rewriting has to be considered (see Section 4.4).

2.2 Order-Sortedness and Polymorphism

Standard many-sorted type structure is too rigid to deal conveniently with a number of practical issues in specification and program design, for instance error and exception handling, subtyping and partiality. Order-sortedness [GM 83], [Gog 84b], [Gog 86], [Poi 86], [GM 87a], [SNGM 89] allows many of these problems to be solved without adding too many complications. In this approach, a subsort relation is imposed on the set of sorts with $s \leq s'$ requiring the carrier for sort s to be a subset of the carrier for sort s', so that a function $f : s' \to t$ is automatically also applicable to values of sort s.

There are a range of issues which have been studied in connection with the order-sorted approach:

1. Deduction in order-sorted algebras

   All the basic results of equational logic generalize to the many-sorted case. However, order-sorted deduction is more subtle and its correspondence with concepts like replacement of equals for equals and term rewriting needs a careful analysis initiated in [GJM 85] and further investigated in [KKM 88], [GKK 88] and [SNGM 89].

2. Exception handling and order-sorted specifications

   Exception handling was one of the original motivations for the development of order-sorted specifications. [GM 83], [GE 83], [GDLE 84] have shown the adequacy of this approach (see Section 3.4).

3. Partiality

   Order-sortedness allows partiality to be handled by making functions total and well-defined on the right subsort. The connections between order-sorted specifications and partiality have been explored in [GM 83], [SNGM 89].

4. Sort constructions

   An essential issue in the order-sorted approach is the way that sorts are constructed. A new supersort can be constructed by including all elements in some existing sort and then enriching the new sort by some additional operators. Or, a subsort can be obtained by adding sort constraints to an existing sort.

5. Methods and tools for theorem proving

   In the last few years, a range of rewrite-based techniques have been developed in connection with order-sorted specifications. This includes algorithms for unification, completion, etc. (see Section 4.4).

Recently, a new approach for obtaining an even more flexible type structure than the one provided by order-sorted specifications, called *unified algebras*, has been proposed in [Mos 89]. In this approach, models are homogeneous algebras in which sorts are treated as values of the algebra. This permits the use of sort construction operations such as union and intersection and makes it possible to deal with partiality and parameterization in a very smooth way. A similar approach, called *equational type logic*, is developed in [MSS 89], [MSS 90]. In this logic, models are standard algebras equipped with a (binary) typing relation, and formulae are positive conditionals with equations and type assignments. A generalization of the idea of order-sorted algebra is described in [KQ 90], where $s \leq s'$ indicates the existence of a (possibly non-injective) coercion function from the carrier for sort s to the carrier for sort s'.

Order-sorted parameterization and parameter passing have been considered in [GMP 83], [Poi 86], [FGMO 87] and [Qia 89]. While order-sorted parameterized specifications turn out to be a simple extension of ordinary parameterized specifications, the notion of order-sorted parameter passing needs to be treated carefully. Two additional questions must be answered in the order-sorted case: how to interpret overloaded (polymorphic) operators and how to interpret the ordering among sorts. Correspondingly, the main problem of order-sorted parameter passing is how to name the newly generated operations and sorts, and how to generate the ordering on these newly generated sorts. A solution is proposed in [Qia 89].

Polymorphism is another very important and related notion. So far, there are four major kinds of polymorphism: overloading, coercion, subtype polymorphism and parametric polymorphism (cf. [CW 85]). The relation of all these kinds of polymorphism to order-sortedness has been discussed in [GM 83]. It is clear that order-sorted algebra is very suitable for subtype polymorphism. It also provides a solution to the other kinds of polymorphism. But some problems are still open, e.g. the relation between parametric polymorphism and parameterized algebraic specifications.

Topics to be Investigated

Most of the topics above need consolidation and further investigation. In particular, the interaction between subsorts and axioms has to be carefully investigated. Adding equations may collapse two sorts and completely change the carrier of the initial algebra. Different semantics for order-sorted algebraic specifications must be considered. With an initial semantics, the transitivity of deduction means that empty sorts have to be prohibited.

With a loose semantics, this restriction can be relaxed, but the notion of validity has to be carefully made precise.

Parameterization in the context of order-sorted specifications is a difficult problem. Semantics of parameterized order-sorted algebraic specifications, semantics of parameter passing, and proof-theoretic characterizations of correct parameter passing have to be worked out.

2.3 Higher-Order Functions and Infinite Objects

Higher-order functions are a concept which occurs in many important applications in computer science. For instance, if a programming language with assignments is treated at a functional semantic level, commands are functions from states to states. The language constructs then correspond to mappings between functions from states to states. If one wants to study recursion, one also has to solve fixpoint equations between commands. Another example are pointer structures which can be very elegantly modeled by higher-order functions. Furthermore, program schemes can be considered as a special form of higher-order functions.

In recent years some attempts have been made to incorporate higher-order functions into algebraic specifications. Möller [Möl 86], [Möl 87] makes an attempt to incorporate higher-order functions in the framework of partially-ordered algebras with monotonic operators. [Qia 90] studies the incorporation of higher-order functions in order-sorted algebras. [TW 86] uses an infinitary least upper bound operator. [Nic 87] gives a rather domain-oriented approach to algebraic specifications including functional domains (cf. also [BBGN 90]). [Bro 86a] tries to incorporate functional sorts into algebraic specifications and, in a similar way to Möller, does not associate the complete function space with a functional sort but rather a subset of nameable (term-generated) functions. These decisions influence the interpretation of quantification. The foundations of a theory of higher-order hierarchical specifications is given in [MTW 88]. The existence of term-generated initial models for higher-order partial conditional specifications has been investigated in [AC 89]. There is a relation to work on typed λ-calculus, such as the theory of constructions [CH 85] and the theory of polymorphism [CW 85]; in [BC 87], [Bre 88], [BG 89] it is shown how equational axioms can be consistently combined with higher-order λ-calculus.

At the moment we are in a situation where we have seen a number of ways to incorporate higher-order functions into algebraic specifications and how to solve the foundational problems associated with them. The next step would be to integrate these ideas into a more comprehensive framework, making a number of design decisions in the process of integration which are governed by the needs of specifications for engineering purposes.

Infinite objects occur in many contexts. For example, the interpretation of circular pointer structures leads to infinite objects. In connection with interactive programs in general, infinite objects are considered. Functions can also be understood as a special form of infinite objects. Infinite objects allow an elegant treatment of certain algorithms using lazy evaluation [BW 88b].

Infinite objects arise in connection with domain theory when complete partially-ordered domains are considered where certain chains converge to infinite objects. Domain theory provides a thorough and extensive theory for domains with infinite objects [Sco 82]. A comprehensive study of infinite objects in algebraic specifications appears in [Möl 85]. An infinite object can be seen either as a result of taking the limit of certain chains or as a directed set of finite objects approximating this infinite object. This is an order-theoretic and in a certain sense non-algebraic view of infinite objects. But infinite objects can also be understood as arising from the solution of certain fixpoint equations, which is an algebraic way of specifying objects. In [BW 83a], [Bro 86a] there are attempts to give a purely algebraic non-order-theoretic approach to algebraic specifications including infinite objects. The construction of infinite objects is closely related to questions of non-strictness (see Section 2.1). Infinite objects arise only if constructor functions are considered for heterogeneous algebras that are non-strict.

Topics to be Investigated

In connection with higher-order functions in algebraic specifications, it has to be investigated which subset of the function space should be associated with a higher-order functional sort. This influences the interpretation of algebraic specifications with respect to model theory and the deductive theory as well as with respect to the interpretation of quantification. Possible candidates are: the full function space, the space of all continuous functions, the space of all monotonic functions or the space of all term-generated functions. Another important issue is the incorporation of a fixpoint operator in connection with higher-order functions. Here there are close relationships to questions of strictness and order-sortedness. The consequences of the different possibilities have to be carefully investigated.

A thorough investigation should be done comparing order-theoretic and equational fixpoint-oriented ways of dealing with infinite objects. An algebraic characterization of infinite objects should be found. The problems in dealing with infinite objects should be investigated especially with respect to questions of term rewriting with infinite objects.

In algebraic specification, the systematic use of recursive definitions sometimes requires unnatural formulations of properties which are intrinsically based on enumeration. In some other cases, it is necessary to introduce auxiliary functions to express iteration or enumeration. It would be interesting to study how to introduce built-in lists together with higher-order operations in algebraic specifications, in order to express enumeration and iteration more easily. One approach that generalises iteration over arbitrary structures is the systematic use of homomorphic extension functionals, see e.g. [Kri 89b].

2.4 Non-Determinism and Concurrency

Non-determinism in algebraic specification may be studied from two different points of view. On one hand, non-determinism may arise during intermediate steps in the specification design process. In that case, the final specification obtained as a consequence of further refinements would be deterministic. On the other hand, some systems have inherently non-deterministic behaviour (for instance, systems of concurrent processes). Up to now, most work done in this field has been related to the second problem. The first problem has been dealt with by means of loose semantics. The only alternative way of handling this problem seems to be [Hes 88].

The most common approach for dealing with non-determinism in algebraic specification [BW 81], [Sub 81], [Nip 86], [AW 89] consists of considering non-deterministic functions as relations, i.e. boolean-valued functions. From a practical point of view, it seems natural that term evaluation should be done just by rewriting as usual (cf. Section 4.4), although such rewriting systems would obviously be non-confluent. The different normal forms obtained when rewriting a given term will correspond to all the possible solutions obtained by a non-deterministic computation. However, when using predicates to describe non-deterministic functions, the evaluation of a term consists in finding the values that satisfy a given relation. This is, in general, more complicated than needed, since it may require the use of narrowing.

A different approach is taken in [Les 82a], in which non-deterministic functions are converted into functions whose arguments and results are sets of values. In fact all operations, in the presence of a non-deterministic function, are converted into this kind of operation. The objectives of that paper are to characterize the class of axioms which do not present problems with respect to this kind of transformation.

The main drawbacks of dealing with sets of values are that either we generalize signatures so that operations may take as operands sets of values, and then we may find the kind of problems studied in [Les 82a] (problems that may be avoided with order-sorted specifications — see Section 2.2), or else the signature becomes too rigid, since it would not be allowed to apply a deterministic operation to the result of a non-deterministic term because of type conflicts.

Recently, Kaplan [Kap 86] has proposed a new approach based on explicitly considering a choice operator. The paper mainly concentrates on the term rewriting aspects associated with these specifications. The main problem of this paper is that the category of models used seems too complicated.

Finally, it must be mentioned that a certain amount of work has been done in the field of algebraic programming language semantics that would be of interest here (for instance [Niv 80], [AR 87d]); see Section 5.2.1 for more on this issue.

Concurrent systems are inherently non-deterministic, so their specification involves all the issues mentioned above. For many other reasons, concurrency is one of the most interesting and difficult subjects for formal specification and formal program development. There are still many unsolved problems concerning its theoretical foundations.

The use of algebraic techniques in concurrency is much emphasized in CCS [Mil 80], CSP [BHR 84], [Hoa 85] and related approaches like process algebras [BK 86] and MEIJE [AB 84]. However, these approaches deal with specialized theories, rather than integrating process modeling and specification into a comprehensive algebraic approach. One of the first attempts in this direction is the work of Broy and Wirsing on the specification of CCS and CSP [BW 83b] within a partial abstract data type framework. Then, both at the theoretical and methodological level, essentially four different viewpoints (with some variations) were explored:

1. combining CCS-like or CSP-like primitives with abstract data type specifications [LOTOS 84], [PA 89];

2. considering processes to be just special data types, the specification of a concurrent system being parameterized on specifications describing the interactions of component processes (the SMoLCS approach [AMRW 85], [AR 87a], [AR 87b], [AR 87c], [AGR 88a], [AGR 88b]); a feature of this approach is that processes, like any other data, can occur in messages exchanged between processes (the higher-order concurrent calculi of [AR 87c] and [AGR 88a]);

3. combining abstract data types with denotational techniques based on stream processing functions [Bro 87a], possibly extended by modal or temporal logics [Pep 87b];

4. combining Petri nets with algebraic specifications [BCM 88], [CJ 85a], [CJ 85b].

The specification and development problem has been considered by Broy in various papers [Bro 85], [Bro 87a], [Bro 87b], [Bro 88] and by Kaplan and Pnueli [KP 87]. In general it seems useful to combine classical abstract data type specification with other techniques (like temporal logic), in order to have property-oriented specifications of dynamic temporal behaviours.

Topics to be Investigated

In spite of some considerable advances, much work remains, both at the foundational and methodological level, in order to have a smooth treatment of concurrency within a comprehensive algebraic approach. We mention especially the following topics:

- understanding which overall algebraic setting is best suited for concurrency (partial, total, continuous, ...);

- algebraic formalization of the various semantics for processes;

- alternative abstract views of processes, not necessarily viewed as labelled transition systems or stream processing functions;

- top-down development, based on a clear notion of implementation and associated with temporal logic techniques;

- rapid prototyping systems (possibly interactive), specially tailored for testing the specifications of concurrent systems.

A basic problem here is that the usual semantic paradigms (initial, final, behavioural) are generally inadequate for expressing interesting semantics for processes. A promising approach seems to be to extend and generalize semantics devised for processes, like bisimulation, testing and others (see [AW 89], [AGR 88a], [GR 89], [AGR 90]).

It is important to find an appropriate framework for dealing with non-determinism. This means finding the best class of models and studying specification and deduction. Also, in order to deal with concurrency, it should be possible to extend the model to cope with partiality and infinite objects. Rewriting techniques which deal with this form of deduction should be developed. The obvious lack of confluence is one of the problems Kaplan has dealt with, by means of a weaker notion. However, his completion procedure only works for left linear systems. Stronger results seem to be needed. Also, it often seems sensible to allow some form of non-termination. It is not at all clear how to obtain good results in this case.

The differences and advantages of the process algebra approach, where concurrent systems are considered as objects in an algebra, and other approaches, where algebraic specifications are given that describe the objects used in concurrency more directly, should be investigated. Different approaches to concurrency have to be considered and the way that algebraic techniques can be combined with those approaches must be examined. The particular semantic properties of concurrent systems such as non-determinism, communication, concurrency and infinite behaviour should be related to topics in algebraic specifications.

In Berlin, a metric approach to continuous data type specifications based on projection spaces and algebras has recently been developed [EPBRDG 87], [EPBRDG 88], [Gro 89] which allows a purely algebraic approach to continuity. This approach should be compared with the well-studied approach of continuous data types based on partial orders. Furthermore this projection algebra approach should be extended to be suitable for a functional semantics of LOTOS-like languages. The relationship to high-level Petri nets combined with algebraic specifications has to be investigated on a theoretical level and also from the application point of view. Another means for describing the behavior of distributed concurrent systems is temporal logic. But to date, temporal and algebraic specifications are based on different approaches to semantic modeling. It must be clarified how these can be amalgamated.

2.5   Institutions

Examples of logical systems in use include first-order logic (with and without equality), Horn-clause logic, higher-order logic, infinitary logic, temporal logic and many others. All these logical systems may be considered with or without predicates, admitting partial functions or not. This leads to different concepts of signature (vocabulary of names), sentence (axiom) and model. There is no reason to view any of these logical systems as superior to the others; the choice must depend on the particular area of application and may also depend on personal taste.

The informal notion of a logical system has been formalized by Goguen and Burstall [GB 84], [GB 86] who introduced for this purpose the notion of *institution*. An institution consists of a collection of signatures together with, for any signature Σ, a set of Σ-sentences, a collection of Σ-models and a satisfaction relation between Σ-models and Σ-sentences. The only "semantic" requirement is that when we change signatures, the induced translations of sentences and models preserve the satisfaction relation. This condition expresses the intentional independence of the meaning of specifications from the actual notation. All the above logical systems (and many others) fit into this mould. Other formulations of general logic having similar motivations but different technicalities include *galleries* [May 85] and Π-*institutions* [FS 88]. Recently, Meseguer [Mes 89] has proposed a generalization of the notion of logical system, much related to the notion of institution, but including a notion of logical calculus, permitting also transformations of one logical system into another.

For purposes of generality, it is best to avoid choosing any particular logical system on which to base a specification approach. This leads to results and tools which can be reused in many different logical systems. For example, it is possible to define specification languages which can be used to build specifications in any institution (examples are CLEAR [BG 80], ASL [ST 88a], OBSCURE [LL 88] and PLUSS [Bid 89]). It is also possible to discuss fundamental concepts such as free constructions [Tar 86a], [Tar 86b], observational equivalence [ST 87a], refinement [BV 87], [ST 87b] and composability of implementation steps [Sch 87b] in this context. Defining a wide-spectrum language in this way (see for example Extended ML [ST 86]) leads to a program-development framework which accommodates not only different styles of specification but also different target languages.

Topics to be Investigated

Some important topics remain to be studied. For example, the approach to specification refinement in [ST 87b] permits different institutions to be used at different stages of the development of a program from a specification. The potential of the technical device used to achieve this flexibility (*semi-institution morphisms*) needs to be more fully explored.

A considerable body of work has so far been developed in the context of an arbitrary institution. But to what extent can this generality be exploited in practice? For example, is it possible to develop components of a program development system (such as specification editors) which really work in an arbitrary institution? How can the institution be plugged in? A notion of *institution with syntax* was formulated in [ST 86] which should deal with obvious problems like the syntax used for sentences.

A basic problem raised by the use of different institutions is to provide methods for transferring results from one institution to another. An attempt in this direction is given in [Mes 89] (the notion of *mapping*); a closely related but more institution-tailored approach, based on a notion of *simulation* of an institution, is presented in [AC 90]. Investigation on this topic is still at an early stage and much further work is needed.

Chapter 3

Development Concepts

The goal and the dream of the algebraic specification approach is the conceptual and methodological support of all levels and major aspects of the system development process as outlined, for example, in [EF 81], [EF 83], [Kre 81c] and [EFH 83b]. In this respect, topics of interest concern the requirements definition, the transformation of specifications, the reusability of components, the handling of exceptional cases and notations for writing specifications. To get a more complete picture, the reader is referred to Section 5.1.

3.1 Requirements Engineering

Requirements engineering characterizes that phase in the system development process where vague wishes about a desired software system are made precise by explicitly stating

- functional requirements ("what is the system to do") and

- non-functional requirements such as

  - quality attributes of the desired functions,
  - requirements for the implementation of the system,
  - requirements for validation, test, maintenance, and installation,
  - requirements for the development process.

Having primarily readability and understandability even for non-expert users in mind, traditional approaches in this area (e.g. SADT, PSL, RSL, cf. [Com 85] for further specific references) incorporate only a few formal concepts and rely mainly on natural language for their semantics. Consequently, they all fail with respect to important aspects such as consistency, completeness, or integrated methodology. Therefore, approaches based on formal models (e.g. algebraic languages, relational languages, or net-based approaches) to requirements engineering have been suggested (cf. e.g. [HK 83], [PP 83], [Par 86], [STW 87]). Experience gained so far with these new approaches, and in particular with the use of algebraic specifications as a conceptual basis, is encouraging. The major idea in this context is based on the observation that in any case a "formalization step" has to take place, and, rather than using a semi-formal language for expressing the original requirements, the formalism for design specifications, viz. an algebraic formalism, should be used from the beginning. This implies a number of consequences, mainly concerning how to describe non-functional requirements and how to support the formalization step, but also how to "explain" the formal specification in terms of more "human" formalisms, such as natural language or graphics. With respect to the informal explanation of formal specifications, some experiences are already available [Swa 82], [Ehl 85]. The crucial aspect here is the process of formalization: since requirements are informal, the transition to specifications cannot be done formally. So there exist only first attempts at methodological recommendations for how algebraic specification concepts can be used for certain purposes [DP 89]. These methodological approaches are backed by a number of case studies [EF 81], [PL 82], [PP 83], [Par 86].

As far as requirements serve as a description of the data processing problem to be solved, one should be aware that such a problem may be specified by the class of all possible solutions (without necessarily knowing a single solution). Therefore, requirements may be formally defined by constraints (cf. Section 1.1) or by using specification languages with loose semantics (cf. Section 3.5). In both cases the semantics of a specification is given by a restricted class of data types, regarded as the acceptable solutions to the problem.

While algebraic specifications seem to cover functional requirements properly, their usefulness for non-functional requirements is less clear and obvious. In this respect, Guttag's, Horning's and Wing's work [GHW 82], [Win 89] is quite promising.

Topics to be Investigated

The idea of using the algebraic specification technique already in the requirements engineering phase of the software development process needs more profound investigation in order to find at least partial answers to the following key problems (cf. also [Par 89]):

- How can a given problem situation be analyzed with respect to identifying the key aspects of the problem and their representation in terms of a conceptual model?

- How can specifications be built incrementally or by modification? In particular, what are the basic specification-building primitives, and what semantic relations are involved?

- How can comprehensibility and understandability be provided for the non-expert, e.g. for the customer of the software to be produced?

- How can one express non-functional requirements within an algebraic specification and verify them during program development?

- To what extent can an algebraic specification language also be used for expressing the development of a specification?

All these investigations should aim at comprehensive methodological support for bridging the gap between an informal problem statement and its formalization as an algebraic specification.

3.2 Transformation of Specifications

Transformation is a theoretically well-founded (cf. [Pep 87a]) and methodologically well-understood technique. It allows the reformulation of specifications into equivalent ones and the conversion of specifications into implementations that are correct by construction. Methods for the transformation of specifications are built on notions of refinement (cf. Section 1.2.3). Specification transformations for specific basic parameterized specifications (records, arrays, etc.) have been studied in [PB 79], [LP 82], [Par 83], [Par 90].

At the level of specification languages, basic laws for module expressions have been developed in [SW 83] for ASL. A related concept is the *module algebra* of [BHK 90]. Laws for module expressions have various operational aspects. One is that of transforming (normalising) module expressions by applying the laws as rewrite rules. In [Die 88] a variation on module algebra is proposed in which the basic modules can be imperatively implemented. Another operational approach is the $\lambda\pi$-calculus of [FJKR 87]. The latter paper is also an application of these ideas to class structures in the sense of object-oriented programming.

Another goal is that of transforming a non-executable specification into an executable one. This goal can be formulated as follows: for a given input vector x satisfying an input condition C, find an output vector z (i.e. the output of some program $P(x)$) satisfying a given input/output relation $R(x, z)$. If R is a logical formula, then the above specification can be considered as a formula of the form

$$\forall x.\, C(x) \supset \exists z.\, R(x, z)$$

called the *specification theorem* (ST). In this case, one way to go from a non-executable specification to an executable one is by proving ST using mathematical induction and extracting a program from the obtained proof. This is known as the *deductive approach* to program synthesis from formal specifications [MW 80].

In logic, there are well-known results about the links between an inductive proof of ST and the recursive definition of the Skolem function P extracted from this proof [Sch 77]. Sato [Sat 79] has shown that if we have a proof of ST, the extraction is performed within intuitionistic logic and the program obtained is correct. Many "program-extractors" were designed within already existing systems [NUPRL 86], or within new systems [Got 79]. How to obtain an automatic or computer-assisted proof of ST becomes the main problem. Kreisel wrote several interesting studies concerning this general topic [Kre 75], [Kre 81a], [Kre 81b], [Kre 85a].

A good deal of work was and is being done within artificial intelligence. Here there are two major lines of research and development:

- building theorem checkers (and program synthesizers) which are able to accept human guidance [NUPRL 86], [GMW 79]

- searching for "special-purpose" automatic theorem-proving methods.

See Section 4.3 for more on the topic of theorem proving.

The pioneering work on deductive program synthesis is that of Manna and Waldinger [MW 80]. They built a formal system within which one can easily and in a natural way justify deductions necessary for proving specification theorems. It is up to the user, however, to decide which deductions must be considered.

Another interesting approach is pursued in the system LOPS [BH 84]. Here the steps to be performed are well-defined, but it is up to the user to perform them in non-trivial cases. This is why, recently, a reimplementation of LOPS has begun based on the above-mentioned "human-guidance" principle.

The approach of Biundo [Biu 86] may be characterized as an intelligent search through the deduction tree. This search is based on a systematic use of matchings. There are limitations with respect to sub-problem synthesis; moreover, only one existentially quantified variable may occur in the specification theorem.

Smith's approach [Smi 85] is based on the application of the *divide and conquer* strategy determined by the recursive construction of objects. Several well-known transformation techniques (e.g. split of post-condition to introduce an invariant, finite differencing) have been implemented in the PROSPECTRA transformation system [Kri 90b].

Dershowitz [Der 85], Kodratoff [KP 83] and Perdrix [Per 86] have advocated the use of completion techniques for the purpose of deriving executable specifications from both the specification of the problem domain and of the requirements for the solution. From the completeness properties of the completion process it follows that an executable specification can always be found, provided that it can be expressed as a canonical system with the given vocabulary and termination ordering. Unfortunately, in most cases auxiliary symbols are needed. It is not clear how to apply completion techniques to the synthesis of functional programs in rewrite rule form starting from requirement specifications of the kind mentioned above. In any case, a good ground completion procedure must be available in order to achieve better termination of such synthesis processes. See also Section 4.4.4.

All the systems discussed so far have in common that they ask the user to solve delicate problems. In contrast to this is the system PRECOMAS (PRoofs Educed by COnstructive MAtching for Synthesis) [Fra 88a], [Fra 88b], [Fra 88c] which does not allow the user to interfere concerning the choice of the deductions to be performed. The method for automatic theorem proving of theorems with existential quantifiers upon which PRECOMAS relies is called *constructive matching* (CM). The main feature of the CM method is that it decomposes the problem of proving theorems into (conditional) equation-like sub-problems which are either directly solved or which can be represented as theorems. These new theorems are then in turn solved in the same way.

Among the systems which provide inductive theorem proving, one should not forget the Boyer/Moore theorem prover [BM 79], [BM 88]. It specializes in doing "clever" generalizations, but it does not prove theorems containing existential quantifiers unless the correct Skolem function is provided.

Topics to be Investigated

Algebraic specifications are assumed to be the starting point for a formal software development process, either based on refinement and verification, on correctness-preserving transformations, or on synthesis techniques.

With respect to refinement, the many notions of correctness have to be compared. Methodological support for generating verification conditions and for carrying out the correctness proofs have to be developed.

In connection with synthesis techniques, the use of completion and other theorem-proving techniques needs more investigation. Clearly one cannot hope for a fully automated synthesis process. Hence an important issue is to integrate automatic techniques into an interactive user-guided process of program development.

3.3 Reusability

The demand for reusability originates from economic considerations and attempts towards standardization. Rather than always starting from scratch, the use of existing components is cheaper and also less error-prone. A central problem for the identification and the correct use of reusable components is the abstract description of such components. A formal specification is the only form of description that can serve as a basis for a correctness proof; it can be processed automatically and it establishes a degree of confidence in the functionality of the component that is particularly important if a component has to be modified before being reused.

Goguen [Gog 84a] proposes the algebraic specification language OBJ as well-suited for the design of reusable software systems. A component's interface is specified as an abstract data type and may be parameterized by other components. Combination of components is possible by instantiation using appropriate fitting morphisms. A similar approach is used in Extended ML [ST 85], [ST 89].

In ACT TWO [Fey 86] components are modules, which consist of two interface specifications, i.e. an export specification and an import specification, and a body specification which implements the export specification in terms of the import specification. Similarly, in LARCH [GH 86c], a component consists of a pair, an "abstract" interface specification and an implementation. Here the implementation is written in a conventional programming language. A similar distinction between a requirement and a design specification is made in PA^{nn}dA-S, the language of the PROSPECTRA project [Kri 90b], based on the notion of visible and private interface in Ada. Ada bodies are generated semi-automatically by transformation.

In the approach of [Mat 84] a component consists of four parts at four different levels of abstraction: a requirement specification, a design specification, a source program and object code. Components are written in a so-called *wide spectrum language* which provides facilities for system design and software development at many levels of abstraction. Matsumoto uses Ada, which has as a consequence that the requirement specification is merely an informal description. CIP-L [CIP 85] and COLD [FJKR 87] are two languages which include algebraic specifications as well as predicative and imperative language styles in one coherent framework and therefore are better suited for such an approach.

In the object-oriented approach of [Mey 87a] a reusable component is represented by a graph of object-oriented programs, each node of which stands for one level of abstraction in the description of the software. In the approach of the ESPRIT-project DRAGON [Wir 88], a reusable component consists of a tree of algebraic specifications, where similarly to [Mey 87a], each node of the tree is an instance of a certain level of an abstraction of the program with the root being the most "abstract" formal specification and the leaves representing the "concrete" implementations. A methodology for reusing components is described in [WHS 89].

A reusability relation has recently been formally defined in [GM 88b]. Here, a distinction between *efficient* reusability and *general* reusability was introduced. Several results on reusability and hierarchy of specifications were stated.

Topics to be Investigated

Algebraic specifications seem to provide a suitable basis for the reusability of software components. In view of this, research should concentrate on:

- development of "libraries" of basic components (as a "standard" repertoire);

- identification and retrieval of reusable components;

- formulation of one component in different formalisms and/or on various levels of abstraction;

- studying the impact of structuring mechanisms (generic modules, parameterized specifications).

Likewise, transformations may serve as a basis for the reuse of (parts of) the software development process (*design reusability*); see Section 5.1.1 and [Kri 88b], [Kri 90b].

3.4   Exception Handling

A well-known difficulty in software development is that the exception handling parts of a system are often the least carefully specified. The specification of exceptional cases and the error recovery policy are done too late, after the specification of the normal behaviour is completed. This results in expensive modifications of earlier design decisions. Thus, a realistic formalism for abstract specifications must take into account all the exception handling features of a system.

Since the pioneer work of [GTW 76], specifying exception handling has turned out to be an especially difficult problem. Some work simply avoids erroneous values (such as the *algorithmic approach* of [Loe 81], [Loe 88] and partial algebra approaches such as [BW 82a]); however they do not entirely treat the exception handling problem because error recovery is then impossible, as erroneous states are avoided. In other work, such as the *operational* approach of [EPE 81], error values are explicitly introduced. These approaches must deal with the *error propagation problem*, viz. how to characterize the value obtained after applying an operation to an erroneous value. In [GTW 76] error propagation is explicitly described with equations. Unfortunately, this approach leads to illegible specifications in which normal cases and erroneous cases are mixed together. However, it demonstrates that abstract data types with errors are equationally specifiable. In [Gog 78a] error propagation is encoded into the models, but it has been shown (in [BG 83] and [Pla 82] among others) that this formalism is not correct. [Pla 82] describes a rigorous treatment based on [Gog 78a]; however all operations must be strict, and strict functions do not allow error recovery. In [Gog 78b] (see also [GM 83] for a more complete version), Goguen suggests considering error propagation as a special case of coercion and overloading in the framework of order-sorted algebras. A recent paper [SNGM 89] suggests a method, called *stratification*, for specifying partial functions in the order-sorted framework. Further investigation will be required to determine whether this approach supports error recovery properly.

Bidoit in [Bid 84] provides a formalism (*E,R-algebras*) which handles error states by means of declarations. It is also possible to declare recovery cases, and an erroneous value will be implicitly propagated in an E,R-algebra except when it matches a recovery case. Unfortunately, classes of E,R-algebras do not in general have initial objects; thus, it is difficult to conduct proofs in these specifications. All the approaches outlined above are based on an explicit introduction of erroneous values, which generate the erroneous part of the algebras. The approach of [BBGGG 85] is a bit more general since recovery can also be explicitly introduced. Another method based on order-sorted specifications is used in [GDLE 84] and [Ber 86], [BBC 86a] by explicitly characterising the OK-values instead of the erroneous ones; these approaches always provide an initial algebra. In [GDLE 84] the signature of a specification distinguishes *safe* operations that cannot produce erroneous values (such as *succ* or + on natural numbers) from *unsafe* operations that may or may not produce erroneous values (such as *pred* or / on natural numbers). On the basis of [GDLE 84] a final algebra semantics has been studied in [Gog 85] where implicit inequations are introduced between OK- and error terms. The approach in [GDLE 84] has been generalized and parameterized in [Gog 87] permitting different kinds of variables for the OK-part as well as the error part of a carrier set. But if all operations are unsafe, then the OK-part of the initial algebra is reduced to a few safe constants. This problem is solved in [Ber 86], [BBC 86a] where OK-values of exception algebras are more carefully specified; moreover this formalism precisely defines a notion of *error messages*. Error messages can be taken into account in the axioms; thus, an extremely wide spectrum of exception handling and error recovery cases can be specified. The abstract implementation problem has also been studied in the framework of exception algebras, and some proof methods have been developed [Ber 86].

In [Kri 86] exceptions and exception handling are dealt with from the methodological side. There they are formally introduced by transformation rules and identified as (abstractly) semantically equivalent to partiality in algebraic specifications and conditionals. The operational semantics is different, however; transformations may lead to efficiency improvements.

Topics to be Investigated

The results obtained so far must be consolidated and extended, e.g. to parameterized specifications, polymorphic types and higher-order types. An open problem is the adaptation of theorem proving techniques to specifications of exceptions.

3.5 Specification Languages

Existing specification languages can be classified according to their underlying logic, semantics or structuring mechanisms. Particularly interesting examples of such languages are CLEAR, LOOK, ASL, ASF, CIP-L, PA^{nn}dA-S, ACT ONE, ACT TWO, LARCH, Extended ML, PLUSS, OBJ3 and OBSCURE.

CLEAR [BG 77], [BG 80], [San 84] was the first algebraic specification language and its influence can be seen in most of the languages developed later. It offered for the first time the now standard operations of combination, enrichment, derivation and parameterization. Its semantics was loose, model-oriented, defined by means of constraints. Its static semantics provided a notion of "environment" that offered a reasonable solution to scoping. CLEAR was the first institution-independent language (see Section 2.5).

LOOK [ETLZ 84], a language designed at IBM and in some sense an ancestor of ACT ONE, had two main aims: simplicity, and compatibility between the semantics at the model and the theory levels. Simplicity was achieved by providing powerful enrichment, combination and substitution operations that would allow explicit parameterization and parameter passing to be avoided. This idea can be found later in LARCH. The second aim, compatibility between the two levels of semantics, was not fully accomplished since no correctness conditions were obtained for the specification building operations. Recently, in [OSC 89] these conditions were finally obtained and exploited in the definition of the GSBL language [CO 88], [Clé 89].

ASL [SW 83], [Wir 86] had as its main aim to provide very powerful specification building operations, in such a way that the language could be used as a *kernel* to design other languages. Because of its aims its semantics is model-oriented. In [ST 84], [ST 88a] it was shown that operations similar to those in ASL can be provided in an institution-independent framework. Extended ML [ST 85], PLUSS [Bid 89] and the meta-language for the semantics of Ada [AdaFD 86] are defined in terms of ASL.

ASF [BHK 89] is based on a pure initial algebra approach. It provides export, import and renaming as specification-building operations. The semantics of these operations is defined axiomatically using module algebra [BHK 90]. The specification part of the wide-spectrum language COLD developed within the ESPRIT project METEOR is strongly influenced by ASF [Jon 89].

CIP-L [CIP 85] is a wide spectrum language that was particularly designed for use within the transformational program development methodology [BPW 81], [Pep 84a], [Pep 84b]. It offers constructs for all levels of program development, ranging from specification constructs via applicative constructs to notations for procedural and machine-oriented programs. For the purpose of formal specification, CIP-L offers a sub-language for algebraic specifications, as well as particular constructs such as set comparison, quantification, choice, and a mechanism for formulating *descriptive* expressions. The characteristics of the CIP-L sub-language for algebraic specifications are (cf. [BDPPW 79], [CIP 81], [CIP 85], [BW 82b], [WPPDB 83]) that it provides parameterized, hierarchically structured specifications, partial operations, first-order axioms and a loose semantics.

$PA^{nn}dA$-S, the specification sub-language of the PROSPECTRA project [KHGB 87], [Kri 87], [Kri 88a], [Kri 90b], [Kri 90c], [BBGN 90] has the same characteristics as CIP-L, extended by higher-order functions, non-strict functions for concurrency with streams, etc. It derives its modularization constructs from the target language Ada. The specification language is also used as a meta-language to develop efficient transformation algorithms and to formalise the development process [Kri 89b], [Kri 90b].

The algebraic specification language ACT ONE [EFH 83a], [EM 85], [Cla 89] is based on the concept of parameterized specifications which includes usual algebraic specification with initial and loose semantics as special cases. The structuring mechanisms for building up larger specifications from smaller pieces are extension, union, renaming, and actualization.

ACT TWO [Fey 86], [Fey 88], the successor of ACT ONE, is mainly based on algebraic module specifications [BEP 87], but includes also basic units for algebraic specifications with loose semantics and constraints, called *requirement* specifications, and for parameterized specifications with initial (functorial) semantics. The structuring mechanisms in ACT TWO are similar to those of ACT ONE but are also defined for module and requirement specifications. The semantics of ACT ONE and of ACT TWO is totally defined on two levels: the first is that of theories, and the second is that of algebras and functors. Under suitable semantical context conditions, the semantics is compositional and global correctness is implied by local correctness.

LARCH [GH 86c] is not really a language, but a family of languages. The so-called LARCH *shared language* is what we may call an algebraic specification language. The main aim of this language is to provide operations for incremental construction of specifications. In order to do this it provides specification building operations similar to those in LOOK [ETLZ 84]. Unfortunately, the formal semantics of this language is not clearly defined.

Extended ML [ST 85], [ST 86], [ST 89] is not tailored to any particular logic. It adopts the modularization mechanisms of the Standard ML programming language [HMM 86], and its semantics is largely expressed in terms of the primitive specification-building operations of the ASL kernel specification language. Extended ML is a wide-spectrum language in the sense of CIP-L, as Standard ML function definitions are just axioms of a certain special (and executable) form.

PLUSS [Gau 84], [Bid 89] is the result of a broad range of experiments in writing large specifications and the treatment of specific institutions within PLUSS has been demonstrated in a series of papers [Des 83], [BCV 85], [BH 85], [BC 85], [BBGGG 85], [Cho 86], [Cap 87], [BGM 89]. The main originality of PLUSS is to maintain a careful distinction between *completed* specification components and specification components *under design*. A completed specification component has the property that its class of possible implementations is fixed. In practice this means that such a specification component is either already implemented or may be implemented without taking regard of its context (for instance, of the other components of a specification in which this completed specification component is used). The semantics of PLUSS is expressed in terms of the ASL kernel specification language.

OBJ3 [GW 88] (cf. OBJ2 [FGJM 85]) is a specification and logic programming language based on order-sorted algebras and logic [GM 83], [SNGM 89]. Within this framework, many of the problems with partiality and polymorphism can be solved. OBJ3 inherits its structuring mechanisms, parameterization and *views* from CLEAR.

OBSCURE [LL 88] is based on module specifications. Each module is interpreted as a function mapping algebras into algebras. Apart from the classical structuring mechanisms, OBSCURE contains operations for the explicit construction of sub-algebras and quotient algebras.

Topics to be Investigated

Arbitrary non-functional requirements are not covered by existing algebraically-based specification languages. Specific aspects, such as parallelism, communication, concurrency, and distributed processing have been studied in [Bro 85], [Bro 86b], [Bro 88] (see also Section 2.4). For other aspects, extensions of the algebraic formalism, e.g., by arbitrary relations (to formulate non-functional relationships between entities) or combinations with other formalisms such as temporal logic (to express time constraints and other issues of real-time processing) might be necessary. Related to the question of how to suitably formulate non-functional requirements is the problem of how to ensure that such requirements are met during program development. This whole area has not yet been seriously touched.

It should be investigated how the various state-of-the-art concepts for expressing modularization, refinement, non-functional requirements, and development strategies can be uniformly combined into a single specification language which moreover supports advanced type disciplines, prototyping and verification techniques. Suitable case studies in specification language design should be undertaken. An important problem in specification language design is parameterization by logics and models, a central motivation for the investigation of meta-concepts such as institutions.

Chapter 4

Support Tools

4.1 Specification Environments and Development Systems

Within the CIP project, a transformation system CIP-S has been designed, formalized using algebraic techniques, and developed into an implementation by means of program transformations [CIP 87], [Pep 87a]. CIP-S supports the application of transformation rules, the reduction of applicability conditions by various verification techniques (including induction), administration of all the different kinds of objects relevant in the development process, and the documentation of all development activities. The design of the system is language independent. An implementation of CIP-S for the language CIP-L is currently being built. Within this effort a strong need for tool support for building, maintaining, editing and analyzing formal specifications has been experienced, cf. [MP 86]. Practical experience leading to a better understanding of the requirements of support tools has been gained [Par 89].

Similarly, in the PROSPECTRA project [KHGB 87], [Kri 87], [Kri 90b], [Kri 90c] the strict methodology of development by transformation from an algebraic specification is completely controlled and supported by a development system. Each kind of activity is conceptually and technically regarded as a transformation of a "program" at one of the system layers. This provides for a uniform user interface, reduces system complexity, and allows the construction of system components in a highly generative way. Development scripts are formal objects that can be manipulated and replayed. There is a uniform approach to program and meta-program development (for transformations in the system) [Kri 89b]; the transformation paradigm is also used for proofs (which are seen as development histories of logical formulae), their replay and re-use, and the development of proof tactics. Apart from interactive specification editors with static semantic checking, the system includes a proof editor and tactic definition system, the CEC subsystem for conditional equational completion [GS 90], and, most importantly, an interactive, extensible transformation component. Specifications, programs, transformation and development rules, scripts and methods, proofs and proof tactics are stored in a development library that supports version and configuration control.

These systems are general in the sense that they are not specifically tailored to the transformation of algebraic specifications.

ASSPEGIQUE [BCV 85], [BC 85] is an integrated environment for the development of algebraic specifications and the management of a specification data base. The aim of the ASSPEGIQUE specification environment is to provide the user with a "specification laboratory" where a range of tools supporting the development and the use of algebraic specifications are closely integrated. The main aspects addressed in the design of AS-SPEGIQUE are the following: dealing with modular, hierarchical specifications, providing ease of use, flexibility of the environment and user-friendly interfaces. The ASSPEGIQUE specification environment supports a subset of the PLUSS [Bid 89] specification language.

The tools available in the ASSPEGIQUE specification environment include a special-purpose syntax-directed editor, a tool to integrate (link together) specification modules, symbolic evaluation tools (including conditional term rewriting, a compiler of conditional term rewriting systems into Lisp code and term rewriting with "built-ins"), theorem proving tools, an assistant for deriving Ada implementations from specifications, and interfaces with the REVE [Les 83] and SLOG [Fri 85] systems. All these tools are available to the user through a full-screen, multi-window user interface and access the specification database through the "hierarchical management tool", which is in charge of maintaining the integrity of the data base. Most of these tools use Cigale [Voi 86], a system for incremental grammar construction and parsing, which has been especially designed in order to cope with coercion, overloading of operators and with a flexible, user-oriented way of defining operators.

The ACT system [Han 88] has been developed to support the specifications of software systems. It comprises an implementation of the algebraic specification language ACT ONE, an interpreter, a persistency checker and a pretty printer. The persistency checker of the ACT system checks sufficient criteria for the correctness of parameter passing of parameterized specifications [EKP 80], [Pad 83], [Pad 85], [Lan 85]. Persistency is needed for the compositional semantics of ACT ONE specifications. Within the SEDOS project some tools for the specification and development of concurrent systems in LOTOS [LOTOS 88] have been designed. The environment for LOTOS comprises a front end for syntax and static semantics checking, a simulator, a prototype compiler and some documentation tools. In the follow-up project LOTOSPHERE it is planned to develop an integrated tool set for LOTOS including verifiers for observational equivalence and generated test sequences.

Topics to be Investigated

Based on reviews of existing development systems, principal components of development environments should be identified and investigated w.r.t. their functionality and mutual relationships. Particular attention should be paid to modularity and extensibility of such systems, as well as to the theoretical aspects of their realization on distributed architectures.

Development environments should be split into logic-independent and logic-dependent parts. A general architecture should be designed, which is as much as possible independent of the logics used and of the associated theorem-proving tools. Moreover, the specific notations of the supported specification languages should be irrelevant to as high a degree as possible.

Any development environment should provide components for some form of "execution" of an algebraic specification (by rewriting, interpretation, or compilation). Here, available results have to be consolidated and improved, mainly to increase the efficiency of prototypes. Further research is needed on:

- rewriting for structured specifications

- rewriting for advanced type systems

- the interaction of rewriting with the execution of compiled components

- compilation by transformation of axioms

- development of abstract machines for rewriting and narrowing

Other important components of a development system are support for validation and verification. Here, existing approaches to validation (including "testing") and ongoing research on various theorem provers should be continued in order to achieve appropriate machine support.

4.2 Executable Specifications and Prototyping

4.2.1 Techniques Based on Rewriting

An increasing number of software engineers consider specifications as very high level prototypes [BW 85]. In addition to or as part of the systems mentioned in Section 4.1, a number of prototyping tools for algebraic specifications have been developed. They are mainly based on term rewriting and narrowing (see Section 4.4). There is an implementation of OBJ2 [FGJM 85] based on the idea of translating order-sorted specifications into many-sorted ones as described in [GJM 85]. An alternative approach which uses specifically designed notions of rewriting and unification for the order-sorted case is described in [KKM 88]. REVE [Les 83] is based on a very sophisticated implementation of the Knuth-Bendix algorithm. The systems SLOG [Fri 84], [Fri 85], [Fri 88] and RAP [Hus 85b], [GH 85], [GH 86a] are interpreters of algebraic specifications using narrowing algorithms. The RAP system has been used for prototyping specifications of the Intel 8085 microprocessor [Ges 89], a simple compiler [HR 89], and the INGRES database system. The CEC system [GS 90] has been built around a new powerful completion procedure [Gan 87b], [Gan 88] for conditional equations. A direct relation between an interpretational and a compilational approach has been given by [EY 87]. Recently, compilers for algebraic specifications have been developed. As target languages appear LISP [Kap 87], Pascal [GHM 87], Prolog [GS 90] and abstract machine code [KI 89], [WB 89a].

4.2.2 Graph Reduction

Graph reduction is a common technique for the efficient implementation of functional programming languages and term rewriting languages (see for example [FK 87] and [Pey 87]). Terms are represented as graphs so that common subterms can be shared, and graph transformation steps correspond to (sequences of) term rewrite steps . While in term rewriting, i.e. tree rewriting, the size of a term may be multiplied in a rewrite step, graph reduction steps enlarge graphs up to a constant bound only. Moreover, representing common subterms only once avoids unnecessary multiple evaluations so that for certain rewriting systems an exponential growth of the length of the derivation can be reduced to a polynomial or even linear growth.

Theoretical frameworks for dealing with graph reduction are given by several authors (see for example [ER 76], [Sta 80], [Pad 82], [Rao 84], [Ken 87], [BEGKPS 87], [HKP 88], [HP 88], [Löw 89]). Topics of investigation are, among others, the correctness of the chosen graph reduction model (with respect to term rewriting) and the preservation of properties of rewrite systems by graph reduction implementations.

Graph reduction is not complete for arbitrary term rewriting systems, that is, the normal forms of certain terms cannot be computed by graph reduction unless expensive additional operations on graphs are considered. Completeness results are provided by [BEGKPS 87] for left-linear term rewrite systems without critical pairs and by [HP 88] for terminating and confluent systems.

In [HKP 88] and [Löw 89] graph reduction rules are considered which allow more general transformations than the simulation of term rewrite steps. An example for the use of such rules is the specification of queues where pointers to both ends of a queue ensure that both insertion and deletion of elements can be performed in a constant number of steps.

Topics to be Investigated

Up to now the speed-up gained by graph reduction has mainly been demonstrated by examples. A precise comparison of the complexity of term and graph rewriting is needed in order to identify classes of term rewriting systems for which graph rewriting is strictly more efficient. Moreover, a theory of parallel graph reduction is missing which provides results about efficient reduction strategies.

4.3 Theorem Proving

For an introduction to theorem proving, [CL 73] is now a classic and [Gal 86] a more recent textbook. Whatever specific logical system one studies, the development of fast theorem provers has to cope with three main problems:

1. The control of the size of the *search space* (also called the problem of *knowledge representation*)

2. The choice of *inference rules*

3. The design of efficient *search strategies*

4.3.1 First-Order Logic

Most first-order logic theorem provers are based on the *resolution* method, in which formulae are represented using a clausal format and resolution is used as the main inference rule. There have been some attempts to use other approaches such as the *mating* method developed by Andrews [And 81] (this is the same as the *connection* method developed by Bibel [Bib 82]). For instance, in the Markgraf Karl Refutation Procedure [Eis 86], the clause set is represented by a graph and the search strategy is an extension of [Kow 70]. In ITP [BLMO 86], several search strategies are implemented, including unit-resolution and set of support, which allow to apply resolution inference to a selected subset of all available clauses. Stickel is developing a Prolog technology theorem prover PTTP [Sti 86]; its strategy, called *model elimination* [Lov 78], is an extension of Prolog's strategy to non-Horn clauses. However, it does not support equational reasoning.

4.3.2   First-Order Logic with Equality

The addition of an equality predicate leads to difficult problems with clausal representation of formulae and resolution-based proof strategies. A solution is to introduce a separate inference rule called *paramodulation* to cope with equality; for instance, both of the above-mentioned theorem provers have a paramodulation rule. They also supply many rules to discard clauses or reduce complex clauses to simpler ones, but most of these rules are efficient heuristics without theoretical foundations. The power of these rules has been established through the extensive development of term rewriting systems, from both experimental [Les 83] and theoretical [Hue 81], [BDH 86] points of view. The Boyer/Moore theorem prover [BM 79] is a fully automatic system which uses highly developed methods for induction. Previously-proved theorems are used to prove new results, so the order in which theorems are presented to the system is critical. The Boyer/Moore theorem prover has been used to prove a wide variety of theorems, including results as difficult as Gödel's Incompleteness Theorem [Sha 86]. Recently, Rusinowitch [Rus 87b] has presented an extension of the Knuth-Bendix completion procedure (see Section 4.4.4) to full first-order logic with equality. In this work, a considerably more efficient superposition rule than paramodulation is shown to be complete, provided a strong reduction ordering on literals exists. Very recently, Rusinowitch's results have been considerably improved by Bachmair and Ganzinger [BG 90a]. They also prove complete a rather general, semantic notion of redundancy for formulas and inferences. The latter seems to be a suitable theoretical basis for the above-mentioned techniques of simplification and elimination of clauses during theorem proving.

Another interesting completion-based technique for first-order theorem proving with equality has been proposed by Hsiang [Hsi 82]. He restricts to the case of unit equations and uses rewriting and completion modulo associativity and commutativity, starting from a canonical rewrite system for the boolean ring.

Section 4.4 presents research on theorem proving specifically devoted to equational theories.

4.3.3   Higher-Order Logic

In Section 2.3, the importance of higher-order specifications is discussed. There is some research on the development of theorem provers for higher-order logic; these include LCF [GMW 79], [Mil 84], [Pau 87], HOL [GH 86b] and Nuprl [NUPRL 86]. There is also an extension of the RAP system for prototyping hierarchical higher-order specifications [Reu 90].

4.3.4   Computer-Aided Proof Checking

In spite of many significant advances on methods for automatic theorem proving, it seems to be obvious now that the goal of a fully automatic general purpose theorem prover is not achievable in the short-term future. A more modest goal is to use the computer as an intelligent proof checker which is able to accept human guidance, pithily expressed, and grind through the symbolic manipulations necessary to check it out.

The LCF theorem-proving system [GMW 79], [Mil 84], [Pau 87] is designed to support a goal-directed style of interactive proof. The user constructs *tactics* encapsulating proof ideas which reduce the goal of proving a theorem of a certain form to a list of sub-goals. Tactics may be combined to produce powerful proof strategies. Although the user is given complete freedom to try any desired proof strategy, including an incorrect one, it is impossible to prove an invalid theorem in LCF. LCF and theorem provers based on LCF have been used to prove theorems involving denotational semantics and functional programming as well as for verifying the correctness of hardware [GH 86b] and to develop programs by proving theorems in constructive logic [NUPRL 86]. Similar ideas have been developed for theorem proving in equational theories with specific applications to algebraic specifications in the context of LARCH [GG 89]. The point of view taken here is that a computer-aided proof must be designed, programmed and debugged. Current directions are now toward better interfaces which use high-resolution screens. The Boyer/Moore theorem prover is a proof checker in effect, since in order to prove a difficult theorem the user must lead the system through the proofs of all the lemmas on which the proof of the theorem depends.

Recent work has attempted to make the same ideas work in a wide variety of logical systems. This is motivated by the need to use different logics for different purposes, including for example first-order logic or equational logic for reasoning about functional programs, Hoare-style logics for reasoning about imperative programs, and logics for reasoning about concurrent systems. The Edinburgh Logical Framework (LF) uses a typed λ-calculus for representing the syntax and proof rules of a logic [HHP 87]. Once a logic has been encoded in LF, checking proofs in that logic reduces to type checking in LF which is decidable. LF has already been used to encode a wide variety of logics [AHM 87] and a prototype implementation based on the Cornell Program Synthesizer is available [Gri 87]. A related approach is that of Isabelle [Pau 86].

Although the underlying motivation for both institutions (see Section 2.5) and LF are the same, connections are subtle and difficult to establish (but see [Mes 89] for some related work). The most fundamental difference is that institutions handle model theory for general logics while LF handles their proof theory. Such connections are required to allow an LF-based theorem prover to be used as a tool in an institution-based program development system. Another interesting issue is the connection between methods for putting together institutions [Tar 85] and methods for putting together LF logics [HST 89a], [HST 89b].

Topics to be Investigated

Theorem proving for a variety of logics is required for program development. Hence, theorem provers should be made logic-independent to a high degree. A careful analysis of the control structures in theorem provers together with the development of a language to describe such structures should facilitate the investigation of new strategies and prepare the design of (perhaps parallel) algorithms for automated deduction. Such a language should provide tools for evaluating control: for instance, it should allow fairness (i.e. no inference is postponed forever) to be checked mechanically.

From such high-level descriptions it should be possible to tailor a theorem prover towards a specific logic to increase its efficiency. To that end, adequate techniques of compilation and partial evaluation should be developed. Instead of representing objects like clauses by data structures and operating on them using a variety of general-purpose algorithms, it is possible to build a special-purpose algorithm for each object and each role it can play. The idea of compiling logic is due to Warren [War 77] who developed it in the context of Prolog.

The logics relevant for program development are rather complex. One should have ways of structuring a logic into "modules" of lower complexity and obtain a theorem prover as a combination of theorem provers for the component logics. Here it also becomes very important to incorporate specialized reasoning rules to deal with particular theories. This should be done in the same framework as resolution (theory-resolution concept of [Sti 86]) and also by using new unification algorithms [Kir 85]. The recent Prolog III language [Col 85] shows the appeal of such a framework.

On the level of specifications and programs there is a similar degree of complexity. To be usable in practice, a theorem prover must be able to handle complex specifications by exploiting their structure; it is possible to use the structure of the specification to localize the search for a proof to an appropriate context [SB 83].

The achievements in resolution-based theorem proving and rewriting-based theorem proving should be combined to mutual benefit. Research should focus on inference rules that limit the growth of the search space and the size of the data (like *demodulation* and *subsumption*) [Rus 87b], [BG 90b], and on backward-chaining strategies that are close to Prolog.

Rewriting- and paramodulation-based theorem proving should be extended to the case of rewriting modulo associativity and commutativity (AC). To establish refutation completeness, a combination of the techniques from unfailing completion and from completion modulo AC is required. At present, these two concepts are developed only under incompatible assumptions about the required reduction ordering on terms [Bac 87].

In theorem proving one is usually interested in the proof of more than one consequence of a given theory. One would like to have available techniques, like completion or partial evaluation, which would allow to "compile" the axioms of the theory such that, at theorem proving time, inferences in which all premises are axioms can be avoided as much as possible. A first step towards this goal has been described in [BG 90b].

4.4 Term Rewriting

4.4.1 Notions of Term Rewriting

Besides the classical notion of rewriting for many-sorted terms (see [HO 80] and [DJ 89] for overviews), new notions have been developed in order to extend classical term rewriting techniques to new application areas.

Conditional Term Rewriting

The origins of conditional rewriting may be found in systems designed for algebraic manipulation such as REDUCE [Hea 71] and SCRATCHPAD [GJ 71]. The first paper dealing directly with this topic was [BDJ 78] which introduced *hierarchical* rewriting, a technique for avoiding non-termination in the evaluation of conditions. Other authors using this technique include [PEE 81], [Rem 82], [Dro 83], [ZR 85]. In [NO 84] the limitations of this technique were studied: it was shown to be incomplete unless some strong version of sufficient completeness is used. The most common approach used nowadays for avoiding this kind of non-termination is to deal with *reductive* systems. This approach was introduced in [Kap 85].

Conditional rewriting may be considered essentially more difficult than usual term rewriting. The reason is that, in this context, knowing whether a term is reducible or not is undecidable [BK 82], [Kap 84].

Two kind of approaches may be distinguished in conditional rewriting: *recursive* and *contextual* rewriting. In recursive rewriting [PEE 81], [Dro 83], [Kap 84], [Kap 85], [JW 86], [KR 89], [Gan 87b], [Gan 88], before applying a rule its condition is evaluated. Then, the rule is only applied if the condition holds. In contextual rewriting, introduced in [Rem 82], a rule may be applied to a term without evaluating its condition. Then the condition is appended to the term as a *context*. This notion of rewriting has been further developed into *clausal rewriting* for clauses with a single positive equality literal in [NO 89].

Order-Sorted Rewriting

To efficiently implement order-sorted specifications, it is useful to have a notion of rewriting in which type checking and computation are treated in a specific way. Order-sorted rewriting is introduced in [GJM 85] and [SNGM 89]. One particular problem that has been addressed is the *sort-decreasing* property of rules — to be compatible with the sort structure, a rewriting step must decrease or preserve the least sort of a term. Decidable criteria for ensuring this property are presented in [SNGM 89], [KKM 88], [GKK 88].

4.4.2 Unification and Matching

Unification or equation solving is as old as mathematics itself. The problem is to find substitutions (values for the variables in an equation) which make both sides of the equation equal.

It is only recently (during the 1960's) that unification has been used in computer science, concurrently with the development of symbolic computation and in particular in work on resolution [Rob 65]. Unification is now at the very heart of present day computing and has a central role in the central processing unit of the fifth generation computer. So the field is now quite large and deep. Detailed reviews of the main methods, results and problems are [SS 84] and [Sie 89] (see also [Kir 85] for the specific problem of equational unification). We summarize here the main directions relevant to the specific interests of this survey.

Unification for Specific Theories

The first explicit account of a unification algorithm was given in Herbrand's thesis [Her 30]. This algorithm, later rediscovered and refined [MM 82], is one of the algorithms most commonly used today. The idea to build properties like commutativity directly into the unification process goes back to Plotkin [Plo 72] who showed how to do this without sacrificing completeness. This opened the way to the general topic of equational (first order) unification where the main milestones are:

1975: associative-commutative unification algorithm [Sti 75], [LS 76], [Sti 81]

1977: decidability of associative unification [Mak 77]

1982: study of decidability of unification problems and first classification [Sza 79], [SS 82], [SS 84]

1985: combination of unification algorithms [Kir 85], [Yel 85], [Her 86], [Tid 86], [Her 87], [Kir 89]; some of these are based on Fage's proof of termination of Stickel's associative-commutative unification algorithm [Fag 84]

1985: automatic derivation of the unification algorithm from a presentation of the theory [Kir 85], [Kir 86]

1987: general combination of unification algorithms [Sch 87a]

1988: combination of unification and disunification problems [CL 89].

Narrowing

Narrowing is a very general unification method which yields a generating set of the set of unifiers, provided that the term rewriting system associated with the equational theory in which equation solving is done is both terminating and confluent. Narrowing is a particular case of paramodulation and is of great interest in logical relational programming languages like EQLOG [GM 86], RAP [Hus 85b], and SLOG [Fri 85]. It was first studied by Fay [Fay 79]. Hullot [Hul 80] showed the link between rewriting and narrowing and gave sufficient conditions for termination of the narrowing process. This was then extended to equational rewriting such as rewriting modulo associativity-commutativity in [JKK 83], which allows equational unification to be considered in an incremental way. For conditional equations, narrowing techniques have been proposed in [Kap 85], [Hus 85a] and [Fri 85].

One of the main problem with to the use of narrowing is its potential non-termination. Recent studies show that the situation is not hopeless and that by restricting the set of nodes in the term to be narrowed, or in factorizing the narrowing tree, the search space decreases drastically [RKKL 85], [Ret 87]. Moreover, the operators' dependency makes it possible to search only in certain directions in the search space [SD 87].

Order-Sorted Unification

The particular problem of order-sorted (equational) unification has only recently been approached. One main difficulty is that even in the case of syntactic unification, the generating set of unifiers is no longer reduced to a single element [CD 83], [Wal 84]. The equational case is more difficult but can be reduced to the single-sorted case for some theories [MGS 89]. The general study of order-sorted unification [Kir 88] and narrowing [SNGM 89] is under development and will probably give better results than methods which translate the problem to the single-sorted case followed by post-processing [Sch 86a].

Disunification

The notion of disunification appeared recently [Col 84] and is of great interest in the context of Prolog and related programming languages. The non-equational framework [KL 87] is extended to the equational case in [Com 88].

Finally, we mention other related research fields that we do not have space to describe fully here: development of a unification chip, for example [Rob 85], and study of higher-order unification [Hue 76].

4.4.3 Termination of Rewrite Systems

Termination [Der 87] is essential for many reasons. By definition, it guarantees that the rewrite mechanism avoids infinite chains. This fact is used as a part of the proof of confluence in the Knuth-Bendix algorithm (see Section 4.4.4). On the other hand, rewrite systems are often used as a description of a program or a set of functions in a specification, where the termination of the rewrite system ensures the termination of the program or of the functions when they are executed. In addition to these points, termination plays an important role in methods for proving the completeness of completion procedures [Hue 81], [HR 87], especially a method called *proof orderings* [BDH 86], [Bac 87].

Classical methods for proving termination are based on orderings on the term algebra. The key idea is to show that a specific noetherian (i.e. well-founded) ordering contains the rewrite relation of which one wants to prove the termination. If such an ordering exists, clearly the rewrite relation terminates. However, instead of proving the inclusion on the whole rewrite relation, one usually localizes the proof by proving that the well-founded relation contains only the rewrite rules; by means of some stability properties, this is extended to a termination proof of the whole rewrite relation. A candidate ordering has to satisfy two properties, namely stability with respect to substitution of terms for variables and stability with respect to the operations. Such an ordering is called a *reduction ordering*. *Simplification orderings* [Der 82], [Les 82b] form an important family of reduction orderings. These are orderings which are stable with respect to the operations of the algebra and are such that any subterm of a term is smaller than the whole term. From a theorem due to Higman [Hig 52] and Kruskal [Kru 60] and applied to this specific problem by Dershowitz [Der 82], these two properties are enough to insure the well-foundedness of the ordering. A recent extension of Kruskal's theorem has opened new ways of building orderings more general than simplification orderings [Pue 86], [Pue 87], [Pue 89].

There are essentially two families of orderings on terms for proving termination. One kind is called *syntactical* and provides the ordering from a careful analysis of the structure of terms. Among these orderings are *recursive path orderings* [Der 82], the *recursive path of subterm ordering* [Pla 78] and the *recursive decomposition ordering* [JLR 83], [Les 84], [KNS 85], see also [Rus 87a]. These orderings are easy to use since they are based on a concept of precedence on operator symbols which is natural, especially in the context of abstract data types. In addition they enjoy a property called *incrementality* which enables the proof of termination to be built "on the fly" during the completion algorithm [FD 85]. Another family of orderings are called *semantical*. The semantical orderings interpret the terms in another structure where a well-founded ordering is known. There are basically two familiar well-ordered sets: the natural numbers and the terms ordered by a syntactical ordering. Taking the first choice leads to considering functions over the natural numbers which insure stability under substitution; since they are simple to manipulate, polynomials [Lan 79] are often used and an implementation of this method can be done [CL 87]. If the set of terms ordered by a syntactical ordering is chosen as a target for the "semantics", this corresponds to a transformation of the rewrite system into another one. For convenience this is described by a rewrite system [BL 87] and properties of commutation have to be checked [BD 86b].

These techniques have been extended to handle termination of equational rewrite systems such as associative-commutative systems. Methods have been proposed based on transformations [BP 85], [GL 86], [Gna 86], [Bac 87] and on polynomial interpretations [CL 87]. A complete survey on the state of the art is [Der 89]. Recently problems of combining terminating rewrite systems were addressed and surprising negative results were obtained [Toy 87], [Rus 87c], [TKB 89].

4.4.4 Completion

The concept of completion for equation systems was introduced by Knuth and Bendix [KB 70]. Its relevance stems from its wide range of applications, including the compilation of equations into a canonical set of "executable" rules, unification, synthesis of programs from specifications, inductionless induction and first-order theorem proving. For an overview and references to original literature see [Der 83], [Der 89]. Milestones in the development of completion procedures are in the work described in [Hue 81], in [BDH 86] and [Bac 87] (see [Les 89] for an implementation based on these principles).

Several authors have proposed correct techniques to minimize critical pair computation [BD 86a]. The concept of proof orderings in [BDH 86] and [Bac 87] provides a very powerful method for proving the correctness of particular implementations of extended or optimized completion techniques. Its spectrum of applications ranges from completion modulo equations [JK 84] to critical pair criteria as collected in [BD 86a] and [Bac 87] from various original papers. Recent research has centered around topics described below.

Completion of Conditional Equations

Completion methods for both approaches to conditional rewriting (cf. Section 4.4.1) have been proposed by several authors. Kaplan [Kap 85] defined the first completion procedure for recursive rewriting. Further developments were made by [JW 86], [KR 89], [Gan 87a], [Gan 87b], [Gan 88]. Completion procedures based on contextual rewriting have been proposed by [RZ 84], [ZR 85], [BR 88], [NO 87a], [Nav 87]. The main problem is that special techniques must be used to avoid failure, since otherwise completion will almost never succeed. The clausal completion procedure proposed in [NO 89] overcomes this problem by using a clausal notation for axioms, combined with powerful simplification rules. In the case of recursive rewriting, the main problem is the treatment of non-reductive equations in which the condition is more complex than the conclusion. An interesting approach to overcome this problem has been described in [Gan 87b], [Gan 88], and [KR 87]. In this work it is proposed to superpose non-reductive equations on their condition by each rule to enumerate the solutions of the condition. This process translates the equation into an equivalent set of reductive rules. Unfortunately this set is infinite in general. However with the techniques described in [Gan 88], in many practical cases termination of the completion process is achieved. These techniques are proved correct by a concept of proof orderings for conditional equations.

A quite different approach to avoid these problems when doing theorem proving from conditional specifications is taken in [Ore 87b]. In this paper, conditional specifications are considered as infinite recursively enumerable equational specifications. This allows standard methods for solving the word problem and for inductive theorem proving to be used.

Order-Sorted Completion

The case of order-sorted logic has been first approached in the non-equational case by [CD 83]. In [GKK 88], [Wal 89], a completion procedure in the framework of equational order-sorted theories is designed and the differences with the standard case are indicated. From a set of axioms, the order-sorted completion procedure builds an equational term rewriting system which is complete for order-sorted deduction. The sort-decreasing property of rules, needed for this completeness, is dynamically checked during the completion. Other specific problems such as orienting an axiom to get a terminating sort-decreasing rule, handling empty sorts or the generation of non-sort-decreasing axioms during the completion process, are also handled.

A different method consists of translating an order-sorted specification into an equivalent many-sorted specification and using a completion procedure for conditional equations. (The translation introduces injectivity axioms for the injection functions between subsorts.) This is done quite successfully within the CEC system [Gan 89]. One immediate advantage is that this method also works for a non-trivial class of order-sorted specifications with conditional and non-sort-decreasing axioms.

Divergence of the Completion Process

According to [BDH 86] and [Bac 87], a completion procedure is a fair strategy for applying a certain set of inference rules to given input equations and rewrite rules.

There are three possible outcomes of a completion procedure. It may succeed and produce a finite canonical rewrite system; it may fail due to problems with the given reduction ordering; or it may diverge, i.e. produce an infinite set of rules. Although the divergence of the Knuth-Bendix procedure was observed in the basic work [KB 70], it was not until the 1980's that the problem was formally considered. Huet [Hue 81] proved that even in the case of non-termination the final infinite rewrite system is confluent, and that the left-hand sides of its rules are pairwise incomparable in the given ordering. [DMT 88] shows that under the fairness assumption, it is not possible to generate a finite complete rewrite system in one case, and enter a divergent process in another case, under the same term ordering, only by changing the critical pair evaluation strategy. Possibilities for avoiding divergence by changing the reduction ordering were studied in [CL 87] and [Mar 87]. A method for testing divergence was proposed in [Les 87] as a modification of a termination test due to [Pla 86]. A strong restriction of the completion procedure to guarantee confluence on terms without variables was studied in [Fri 86]. His restriction is due to the potential divergence of the general completion process. Sufficient conditions for a divergence test, developed as a study of structural properties of rewrite systems, were introduced in [HP 86], with the notion of *crossed rules*. These issues were also handled in

[MP 88]. Further detailed study of structural properties of rules, with the goal to relax the conditions so that they would cover a more general class of divergent rewrite systems, was undertaken in [Her 88] and is still in progress. A general theory for coping with divergent rewrite systems in a finite way was developed by Kirchner [Kir 87].

Inductive Reducibility and ω-Completeness

As proved by Birkhoff, equational logic is complete in the sense that if an equation is valid in all the models of an equational theory (called a *variety*) it can be proved by equational reasoning. However, no complete proof system can exist for validity of equations in the initial model of an equational theory, even if induction is added, as shown in [MS 85]. Stronger results (incompleteness even for ground equations) were obtained for equational theories plus data constraints, and for equational theories plus hierarchy constraints.

In algebraic specifications, several kinds of completeness are especially important. Among them is sufficient completeness, i.e. checking that an operator is fully defined [GH 78], [NW 83], [Thi 84]. Sufficient completeness is a specific case of a more general property, namely *inductive reducibility* or *ground reducibility*. A term is ground reducible if all its ground instances are reducible. Sufficient completeness for f is then ground reducibility of the term $f(x_1, \ldots, x_n)$. Algorithms for ground reducibility were proposed in [Pla 85], [JK 86], [KNZ 87] and [Com 88]. No implementation exists and nothing is known about the efficiency of the algorithm in the general case.

Another problem which is important especially in proof by consistency [KM 87] is ω-*completeness* or *inductive completeness* [Pau 84], [Hee 86], [LLT 86]. A set of equations is ω-complete when a theorem is valid in any model (or provable by equational reasoning) if and only if it is valid in the initial model. In such theories there is no need for proofs by induction, equational reasoning is enough. This subject was originally begun by Tarski. This property is very difficult to check for equational specifications [Hen 77]. However, we would expect it to be easier to prove for a term rewriting system, at least for a class of systems large enough for application to algebraic specifications, and many useful examples exist where the proof is not too difficult.

Topics to be Investigated

In the area of term rewriting, the power and efficiency of classical techniques for termination proofs, termination of completion, narrowing, unification algorithms and (inductive) proofs by consistency need to be increased. At the same time, these techniques have to be extended to handle conditional equations and full first-order logic as well as more advanced type disciplines.

Chapter 5

Applications

5.1 Software Development Process

It is widely recognized that formal development of correct programs cannot be undertaken without proper formal support. The algebraic approach to program development has good formal foundations and provides a rigorous approach to program development. Algebraic techniques may in particular serve as a formal support for the early phase of a software project (specification). Moreover, it is well-known that the decomposition of large systems into adequate modules is supported by the concept of abstract data type which is basic in algebraic specifications.

The algebraic framework provides formal criteria for the verification of development steps, and equational logic supplies powerful tools for machine-supported deduction and therefore for rapid prototyping of specifications, proofs and tests. Algebraic methods support program development from formal specification to efficient implementations: program transformations are usually based on algebraic techniques, efficiency oriented and control flow oriented concepts can be modeled in an algebraic framework and supported by algebraic techniques.

The algebraic approach has been widely used and intensively studied within the CIP project where a methodology for program development by transformations has been developed (cf. e.g. [BPPW 77], [BPPW 78], [BP 81], [BP 82], [BW 82b], [CIP 85], [PP 86]). The ESPRIT project PROSPECTRA is based on this work ([KHGB 87], [Kri 87], [Kri 90b], [Kri 90c]). It plays also a crucial role within the ESPRIT project METEOR where algebraic specifications form the basis of an object-oriented methodology of program development. In the specification language PLUSS [Gau 85], [Bid 89], linguistic support is provided for the development of algebraic specifications.

The formal notion of implementation of algebraic specifications and the correctness criteria for such implementations form a basis for the stepwise construction of programs. A particular way of developing a program is to compile a specification of a certain form directly into efficient code [Kap 87].

The development of a methodology for "algebraic programming" [Han 86] is needed on all levels of the software construction process: development of formal specifications from requirements; analysis and validation of formal specifications; transformation and implementation of specifications via specifications of a more concrete form for which the transition to efficient programs is possible. This methodological level should be supported by two other levels: a conceptual level on which the design of relevant structural properties of algebraic specifications such as hierarchical consistency or sufficient completeness are studied, and a technical level which provides verification techniques for algebraic specifications such as induction proofs, normal form proofs or Knuth-Bendix completion. All these points have already been addressed in Chapters 3 and 4.

5.1.1 Formalization of the Development Process

Various authors have stressed the need for a formalization of the software development process: the need for an automatically generated transcript of a development "history" to allow re-play upon redevelopment when requirements have changed, containing goals of the development, design decisions taken, and alternatives discarded but relevant for redevelopment [Wil 86], [SS 83]. A development script is thus a formal object that does not only represent a documentation of the past but is a plan for future developments. It can be used to abstract from a particular development to a class of similar developments — a development method, incorporating a certain strategy. Approaches to formalize development descriptions involve a form of development program [Wil 86], regular expressions over elementary steps [Ste 82], functional abstraction [FJOKRR 87], and composition of logical inference rules [Sin 87], [JHW 87].

In the PROSPECTRA project [KHGB 87], [Kri 87], [Kri 90b], [Kri 90c], an elementary development step is the application of a single program transformation rule. A development script is then a sequence of rule applications. The question is how best to formalize rules and strategies. The approach taken in [Kri 89b], [Kri 90c] is to regard transformation rules as equations in an algebra of programs, to derive basic transformation operations from these rules, allowing composition and functional abstraction, and to regard development scripts as (compositions of) such transformation operations.

Using all the results from program development based on algebraic specifications, we can then reason about the development of transformation programs or development scripts in the same way as about programs. For example, we can reason about development goals as requirement specifications for transformation operations in the syntactic algebra and characterize them as structural normal forms; we can implement transformation operations in various ways and optimize them using algebraic properties; we can use composition and functional abstraction; in short, we can develop correct, efficient, complex transformation operations from elementary rules stated as algebraic equations. Moreover, we can regard development scripts as formal objects, i.e. as (compositions of) such transformation operations. We can specify development goals, implement them using available operations, simplify development terms, re-play developments by interpretation, and abstract to development methods, incorporating formalized development tactics and strategies. The abstraction from a concrete development to a method and the formalization of programming knowledge as "transformation rules + development methods" will be a challenge for the future.

5.1.2 Applications Within the Development Process

As previously discussed, algebraic specifications can be useful not only at the specification stage, but also at almost all stages of the usual software development process. Uses include prototyping (see Section 4.2), program construction by refinements or transformations (see Section 3.2), and proving correctness of programs. Algebraic specifications can also be used as a basis for functional testing of programs.

A theory of software testing, based on formal specifications, was proposed by Bougé, and then applied to algebraic specifications. The basic ideas are the following [BCFG 86]:

- Given the axioms of an algebraic specification, which are equations (possibly positive conditional), the left-hand side and the right-hand side of each equation are evaluated using the program under test, for "interesting" values of the variables. The success or the failure of the test is decided by checking that both results are equivalent.

- the structure of the specifications is used to guide the choice of the test data (i.e. the "interesting" values above). For instance, a complexity measure can be defined on some sorts, every premise of each equation must be valid at least once, etc.

Recently, some coverage criteria for algebraic specifications have been defined [GM 88a]. These criteria induce incremental test strategies, where the limit of the testing process is a correctness proof of the program.

These testing strategies can be expressed formally. Thus, there is some hope that they can be automatized using theorem proving techniques. At this moment, experiments are performed using logic programming and its extensions (SLOG [Fri 85], RAP [GH 85]).

In [Cho 87] an approach to integration testing with prototyping was proposed: starting with a hierarchical and modular executable specification of the system to be realized, implemented modules are progressively integrated in place of the corresponding specified modules. Performing an execution of such a system, where the integration is partial, requires mixing evaluation in the specification language and in the programming language used in the implemented modules.

Topics to be Investigated

The various possibilities of using algebraic specifications at stages of the development process other than specification must be explored, consolidated and coordinated: rapid prototyping, user interfaces [EFH 85], reuse of program modules, proving program correctness, testing specifications and programs.

5.1.3 Software Modularity

Modularization is one of the main principles in software development. The aim is to divide the task of developing a large system into modules which can be developed independently of each other.

In an abstract view, a module comprises three main components: its interface, its internal construction, and its externally-visible behaviour. These components of a module are given syntactically as well as semantically, and form a conceptual unit. Modular systems are comprised of modules which are composed in a particular way using interconnection mechanisms and combinators provided by the modularization framework in use. The design of a module specification, the choice of modularization, and the design and development of a modular system are tasks which can never be fully mechanized or formally solved

[WE 86]. Such tasks require skill, experience and imagination. But because of this it is important to have support in various ways.

The basic questions for a theory of specification of modules and modular systems concern mainly the following topics:

- Concept of module specifications and modular systems adequate for software system design and development;

- Correctness of module specifications;

- Compositionality of module operations;

- Equivalence of different modular structures of a system;

- Implementation and refinement of modules and modular systems.

Various module concepts, which are described in Section 1.2.2, have been designed in the field of algebraic specification to cover various phases of software development, fulfilling the above criteria to a greater or lesser extent.

Topics to be Investigated

The relationship between specification modularity and program modularity is of first importance and must be studied, as well as the evolution of the decomposition of a system into components during its development (compatibility of horizontal structuring and vertical development).

5.2 Programming Languages

5.2.1 Semantics of Programming Languages

Algebraic specifications can be successfully applied to specify the semantics of programming languages. This is a worthwhile approach since it permits a proper description of the meaning of programming languages with all the advantages algebraic specifications have when they are used for the description of data structures. They allow a model-independent, property-oriented description of programming languages without forcing the understanding and knowledge of a particular mathematical model.

In recent years, work has been done within the area of the semantic description of programming languages by algebraic techniques (apart from the field of concurrency already mentioned — see Section 2.4) mainly by Mosses under the keyword of *abstract semantic algebras* [Mos 83]. Further work has been done by the ADJ group in the course of an attempt to provide a foundation for the application of algebraic specifications to compiler construction [TWW 79], by Wand in giving algebraic descriptions of functional languages [Wan 80] and by Broy and Wirsing and also by Pepper in giving an algebraic theory based on the concept of partial algebras for a semantic specification of programming languages [Pep 79], [BW 80], [BPPW 80], [BPW 80], [BPW 87]. This work has shown clearly that a purely algebraic description of programming languages is possible and helpful in analyzing programming languages and their semantics.

In recent years a very challenging problem has been to define the semantics of languages with strong interference from sequential (imperative) and concurrent constructs, Ada being the most important representative in this class (see [AGMRZ 86]). By using the algebraic techniques for the specification of concurrent systems developed in the SMoLCS approach, it was possible to give the first full formal definition of Ada [AdaFD 86]. The foundations of this approach to semantics are in [AR 86] and [AR 87d]. Two notable points are that the overall definition of Ada is just one (highly structured) algebraic specification, with an appropriate semantics; moreover the special meta-language devised for the definition can be translated into the kernel algebraic specification language ASL [SW 83], [Wir 86].

A partly open problem is to extend current techniques to deal with object-oriented languages (see Section 5.2.4). Since such languages involve notions of class and inheritance, which are of interest in their own right, it seems natural to adapt algebraic techniques for formalizing these basic constructs. An attempt in this direction is [GM 87b]. A more recent attempt, handling also dynamic sharing and concurrent features, is [BZ 89]. But still the final word has not been said, and probably the best solution is to be found in a close connection between object-oriented semantics and object-oriented specification techniques.

Topics to be Investigated

Since the foundations for an algebraic description of programming languages are already in place, the next step should be to develop these techniques into more practical tools for the description of complex language constructs. A good example of such work is the research of Mosses who tries to isolate and classify a number of semantic properties of programming language constructs using algebraic specifications. Another important issue is to reduce the gap between semantics of programs and their specification/verification. This is especially important for languages used in practice, where programs can hardly be seen as specifications.

5.2.2   Functional Programming

Functional programming and algebraic specifications are closely related. In algebraic specifications, families of functions are introduced and specified by means of conditional equations. In functional programs, functions are defined by a combination of language constructs based on a number of built-in functions which are combined using if-then-else, function abstraction, and a fixed point operator. In a sense, if a sufficiently powerful algebraic specification language is used, functional programming can be seen as a sub-style of algebraic specifications.

A great deal of work has been done in the area of functional programming in recent years, including the development of powerful functional programming languages, such as FP [Bac 78] and Standard ML [HMM 86]. A term rewriting treatment of functional programs is available (see Section 4.4). Implementation techniques for functional programs have been carefully considered, and special machine architectures have been developed for the implementation of functional programming languages. Therefore, a functional programming language provides an excellent target language for the development of programs from algebraic specifications.

Functionals (or higher-order functions, see Section 2.3) often reduce the effort for program development significantly and serve as a kind of "program generator". The technique of homomorphic extension functionals (and their specialisation) is important in this context (cf. e.g. [Kri 89b]). Algebraic axioms for higher-order functions are a powerful specification method (cf. e.g. the theory of lists in [Bir 89]) and provide a basis for formal reasoning about functional programs.

Topics to be Investigated

Functional programming should be incorporated into the framework of algebraic specification as a particular sub-style for which special proof rules and special term rewriting rules are available. However, the incorporation of such a sub-style only seems possible if non-strict functions are included as well as a flexible way to write combining forms for functional programs.

5.2.3 Logic Programming

As mentioned in Section 2.5, a wide-spectrum language with an institution-independent semantics provides the basis for a program-development framework which accommodates not only different styles of specification but also different target languages. Such a language is Extended ML [ST 85], [ST 86], [ST 89], an extension to Standard ML [HMM 86] whereby axioms are allowed in module interface declarations and in place of code in module definitions. In this framework, programs are viewed as axioms of a special form. Thus, if the usual institution is replaced by one in which axioms include at least Horn clauses, the result is a framework for stepwise formal development of modular Prolog programs.

A module system for Prolog based on the one in Extended ML has already been developed [SW 87]. The semantics was obtained directly from the institution-independent semantics of Extended ML as indicated above, although for the sake of readability the general category-theoretic constructions in the semantics were replaced by simple set-theoretic ones. There seems to be no reason why work on formal program development in the Extended ML context cannot be directly translated to Prolog in a similar fashion.

Topics to be Investigated

It is not clear that the same issues are relevant in developing Prolog programs as in developing programs in functional or imperative languages. For example, it seems that Prolog programs are typically not very "data-oriented", at least in comparison with programs written in a modern functional language like Standard ML. What are the implications of this for a formal program development method which is mainly aimed toward refinement of data representations?

5.2.4 Object-Oriented Programming

Object-oriented programming is a programming style which emphasizes the description of data structures instead of the description of algorithms. This style originated with SIMULA-67 [DMN 70], in which most of the features of later object-oriented languages can be found. Well-known recent object-oriented languages include SMALLTALK-80 [GR 83].

Object-oriented programming can be defined as a style in which a system is described as a collection of *objects*. The internal data of an object cannot be accessed directly by other objects; instead, objects interact by calling *methods* (in Smalltalk terminology), i.e. sending messages to each other. Objects are dynamic entities which can be created during the execution of a program, and which can have an internal activity of their own (in parallel with the activities of other objects).

An object is not directly defined but is an instance of a *class*; objects in the same class all have the same set of variables and execute the same methods in response to messages. An important relation between classes is the *inheritance* relation; a class inherits from another its variables and its methods; new variables and new methods can be added, possibly overriding existing variables and methods. In pure object-oriented languages as Smalltalk-80, classes are also seen as objects, which react to messages by creating an instance of themselves.

After a very application-oriented phase during which several software systems have been produced (first the Smalltalk-80 programming environment, which then inspired a whole generation of environments sharing the common idea of a visual interactive object-oriented user interface — SunWindows, the Macintosh Toolbox, Microsoft Windows, etc.), the scientific community has recognized the need for a formal basis for this approach. Work on applications continues, both on the development of object-oriented languages (new languages, such as e.g. Eiffel [Mey 87b], whose aim is to combine object-oriented concepts with a more traditional view of software engineering, as well as old languages integrated with object-oriented features, like Object Pascal, Objective C [Cox 86] and MacApp [Sch 86b]) and on the analysis of key concepts (e.g. inheritance vs. delegation [Lie 85]). From the theoretical point of view, many recent attempts have been made at giving a formalization of object-oriented languages; these include a formal semantics of Smalltalk-80 [Wol 87] and attempts [GM 87b] at unifying functional, logic and object-oriented programming.

Topics to be Investigated

In view of the increasing number of software systems which are based, either directly or indirectly, on object-oriented concepts, it is clear that the object-oriented style represents a revolutionary change in the attitude of programmers (and of end-users), since it introduces a way of thinking of a system from a point of view which is quite different from the usual "algorithm based" one. At the research level, even though a strong effort has been made recently on these topics and it seems possible to give a reasonable formalization of existing features with existing techniques, what seems to be missing is a new "object-oriented" theoretical framework in which the new concepts (such as object, inheritance, delegation and so on) would be given a proper assessment.

There is one especially challenging aspect of the algebraic treatment of object-oriented features: objects are dynamic entities and so the usual static aspects of abstract data types techniques have to be extended. Probably some techniques from the algebraic treatment of concurrency should be borrowed (e.g. viewing objects as processes).

Finally, an open problem is the development of formal methodologies for the design phase of an object-oriented system starting from an abstract specification.

5.3   Databases and Knowledge Bases

In the design of databases, information systems and knowledge bases, the conceptual modeling of information to be stored plays an important role. Up to now, little work has been done to support conceptual modeling by algebraic tools or other formal methods. Exceptions are the applicative approach of [EKW 78], [EKW 79], [Fey 80], [DMW 82] and the modal systems of algebras of [GMS 83], [KMS 85].

The importance of formal semantics for programming languages was recognized already in the 1960's. Since then, formal methods have had an important influence on the design of new programming constructs and modern languages. In the field of database languages (usually equipped with at least a schema and a query part) it is an exception [SM 87] when a language is defined in mathematically precise terms. More common is the definition of "semantics" by means of examples. The state of the art is more or less intuitive and has not yet reached the level of precision achieved in the area of programming languages. One of the reasons for the lack of formal descriptions of (especially) relational database languages is probably the fact that classical formalisms like relational algebra or relational calculus are not powerful enough to explain certain features of query languages, e.g. aggregate functions. Therefore a more comprehensive approach is needed.

Translations between database languages have been considered to some extent during the past few years, but only from a concrete implementation viewpoint [Bue 87]. For example, the central part of some languages is defined by translation into the relational algebra which is often taken as an implementation basis [CG 85]. But due to the lack of formal semantics and due to the weakness of relational algebra, no systematic approach was possible. It is also often the case that a "user-friendly" language is considered to be only a front end for a more expressive and "harder to use" language, e.g. QBE is often offered as a front end for SQL-systems.

In [SSE 87], [SFSE 89], [ESS 89a], [ESS 89b], several aspects of an object-oriented approach to information system specification and design are analysed, covering both structural and dynamic aspects, and the kernel for an algebraic/categorical theory of abstract object specification is provided. These research activities are supported by the ESPRIT BRA Working Group ISCORE (Information Systems: Correctness and Reusability). This project aims at the development of logical and semantic foundations, methodology, languages, and software tools. The semantic domain is provided by a category of objects in the sense of object-oriented programming, where morphisms describe interaction between objects and colimits describe their parallel composition.

Topics to be Investigated

Formal concepts for database and knowledge base specification have to be developed, including a mathematical model of "knowledge", catering for abstract and modular specifications. Both database (resp. knowledge base) schema and the associated transactions have to be described by rigorous algebraic semantics [SS 85], [SS 87], [FSS 88].

In order to compare different languages and models for data, attention has to be paid to the formal semantics of both. Due to its uniformity and expressiveness, the algebraic framework seems to be an ideal candidate to describe all features offered by the various models and languages.

When the algebraic semantics of these languages is well-understood, it will be necessary to study their mathematical properties and to compare their expressiveness in a precise way. Also, the question of formal translations between different approaches must be considered.

Bibliography

The reference list is in alphabetical order according to citation names rather than according to author names. Please note that citation names such as [And 81], which are used for references with a single author, precede citation names such as [AB 84], which are used for references with multiple authors.

The following abbreviations are used:

LNCS *nn*   =   Lecture Notes in Computer Science, Vol. *nn*
IFB *nn*   =   Informatik-Fachberichte Vol. *nn*

[AdaFD 86]   E. Astesiano, C. Bendix Nielsen, N. Botta, A. Fantechi, A. Giovini, P. Inverardi, E. Karlsen, F. Mazzanti, J. Storbank Pedersen, G. Reggio, E. Zucca: The draft formal definition of ANSI-MIL/STD 1815A Ada. Deliverable 7 of the CEC-MAP project (1986).

[And 81]   Peter B. Andrews: Theorem proving via general matings. *Journal of the Assoc. for Computing Machinery* 28(2), 193–214 (1981).

[AB 84]   D. Austry, G. Boudol: Algèbres de processus et synchronisation. *Theoretical Computer Science* 30 (1984).

[AC 89]   E. Astesiano, M. Cerioli: On the existence of initial models for partial (higher-order) conditional specifications. *Proc. Joint Conf. on Theory and Practice of Software Development*, Barcelona. Springer LNCS 351, 74–88 (1989).

[AC 90]   E. Astesiano, M. Cerioli: Commuting between institutions via simulations. Technical report, Formal Methods Group, University of Genoa (1990).

[AGMRZ 86]   E. Astesiano, A. Giovini, F. Mazzanti, G. Reggio, E. Zucca. The Ada Challenge for new formal semantic techniques. *Proc. of the Ada-Europe 1986 Intl. Conf. on Ada: Managing the Transition*. Cambridge Univ. Press, 239–248 (1986).

[AGR 88a]   E. Astesiano, A. Giovini, G. Reggio: Generalized bisimulation in relational specifications. *Proc. 5th Symp. on Theoretical Aspects of Computer Science*. Springer LNCS 294 (1988).

[AGR 88b]   E. Astesiano, A. Giovini, G. Reggio: Data in a concurrent environment. *Proc. Concurrency '88 Conference*, Hamburg. Springer LNCS 335 (1988).

60

[AGR 90]   E. Astesiano, A. Giovini, G. Reggio: Observational semantics and observational logic. Technical report, Formal Methods Group, University of Genoa (1990).

[AHM 87]   A. Arnon, F.A. Honsell, I.A. Mason: Using typed lambda calculus to implement formal systems on a machine. Report ECS-LFCS-87-31, Univ. of Edinburgh (1987).

[AMRW 85]   E. Astesiano, G.F. Mascari, G. Reggio, M. Wirsing: On the parameterized algebraic specification of concurrent systems. *Proc. Joint Conf. on Theory and Practice of Software Development*, Berlin. Springer LNCS 185 (1985).

[AR 86]   E. Astesiano, G. Reggio: A syntax-directed approach to the semantics of concurrent languages. *Proc. IFIP Congress 1986*. North-Holland, 571–576 (1986).

[AR 87a]   E. Astesiano, G. Reggio: The SMoLCS approach to the formal semantics of programming languages: a tutorial introduction. *Proc. CRAI Intl. Spring Conf. on Innovative Software Factories and Ada*. Springer LNCS 275 (1987).

[AR 87b]   E. Astesiano, G. Reggio: An outline of the SMoLCS methodology. *Mathematical Models for the Semantics of Parallelism*. Springer LNCS 280 (1987).

[AR 87c]   E. Astesiano, G. Reggio: SMoLCS driven concurrent calculi. *Proc. Joint Conf. on Theory and Practice of Software Development*, Pisa. Springer LNCS 249 (1987).

[AR 87d]   E. Astesiano, G. Reggio: Direct semantics for concurrent languages in the SMoLCS approach. *IBM Journal of Research and Development*, 31(5) (1987).

[AT 82]   P.R.J. Asveld, J.V. Tucker: Complexity theory and the operational structure of algebraic programming systems. *Acta Informatica* 17, 451–76 (1982).

[AW 89]   E. Astesiano, M. Wirsing: Bisimulation in algebraic specifications. *Proc. Colloq. on Resolution of Equations in Algebraic Structures*, Austin. Academic Press (1989).

[Bac 78]   J. Backus: Can programming be liberated from the von Neumann style? A functional style and its algebra of programs. *Comm. of the Assoc. for Computing Machinery* 21(8), 613–641 (1978).

[Bac 87]   L. Bachmair: Proof Methods for Equational Theories. Ph.D. thesis, Univ. of Illinois at Urbana-Champaign (1987).

[Ber 86]   G. Bernot: Une sémantique algébrique pour une spécification différenciée des exceptions et des erreurs: application à l'implémentation et aux primitives de structuration des spécifications formelles. Thèse de troisième cycle, Université de Paris-Sud, Orsay (1986).

[Ber 87]   G. Bernot: Good functors ... are those preserving philosophy. *Proc. Summer Conf. on Category Theory and Computer Science*, Edinburgh. Springer LNCS 283, 182–195 (1987).

[Bib 82]   W. Bibel: *Automated Theorem Proving*. Vieweg-Verlag, Braunschweig (1982).

[Bid 84]   M. Bidoit: Algebraic specification of exception handling and error recovery by means of declarations and equations. *Proc. 11th Intl. Colloq. on Automata, Languages and Programming*. Springer LNCS 172, 95–108 (1984).

[Bid 88]   M. Bidoit: The stratified loose approach: a generalization of initial and loose semantics. *Recent Trends in Data Type Specification, Selected Papers from the 5th Workshop on Specification of Abstract Data Types*, Gullane, Scotland. Springer LNCS 332, 1–22 (1988).

[Bid 89]   M. Bidoit: PLUSS, un langage pour le développement de spécifications algébriques modulaires. Thèse d'Etat, Université Paris-Sud, Orsay (1989).

[Bir 89]   R. Bird: Lectures on constructive functional programming. In: *Constructive Methods in Computing Science* (M. Broy, ed.). NATO ASI Series F55, 151–218, Springer (1989).

[Biu 86]   S. Biundo: A synthesis system mechanizing proofs by induction. *Proc. 1986 European Conf. on Artificial Intelligence*, 69–78 (1986).

[Bre 88]   V. Breazu-Tannen: Combining algebra and higher-order types. *Proc. 3rd IEEE Symp. on Logic in Computer Science*, Edinburgh (1988).

[Bro 85]   M.Broy: Specification and top down design of distributed systems. *Proc. Joint Conf. on Theory and Practice of Software Development*, Berlin. Springer LNCS 185 (1985).

[Bro 86a]   M. Broy: Partial interpretations of higher order algebraic types. Lecture Notes of the International Summer School on Logic of Programming and Calculi of Discrete Design, Marktoberdorf (1986).

[Bro 86b]   M. Broy: A theory for nondeterminism, parallelism, communication and concurrency. *Theoretical Computer Science* 45, 1–61 (1986).

[Bro 87a]   M. Broy: Views of queues. Report MIP-8704, Universität Passau (1987).

[Bro 87b]   M. Broy: Algebraic and functional specification of a serializable database interface. Report MIP-8718, Universität Passau (1987).

62

[Bro 88]   M. Broy: An example for the design of distributed systems in a formal setting: the lift problem. Report MIP-8802, Universität Passau (1988).

[Bue 87]   G.Bueltzingsloewen: Translating and optimizing SQL queries having aggregates. *Proc. 13th Conf. on Very Large Data Bases* (1987).

[Bur 86]   P. Burmeister: *A Model Theoretic Oriented Approach to Partial Algebras.* Akademie-Verlag (1986).

[BBC 86a]   G. Bernot, M. Bidoit, C. Choppy: Abstract data types with exception handling: an initial approach based on a distinction between exceptions and errors. *Theoretical Computer Science* 46(1), 13–46 (1986).

[BBC 86b]   G. Bernot, M. Bidoit, C. Choppy: Abstract implementations and correctness proofs. *Proc. 3rd Symp. on Theoretical Aspects of Computer Science.* Springer LNCS 210, 236–251 (1986).

[BBDPPW 82] F.L. Bauer, M. Broy, W. Dosch, H. Partsch, P. Pepper, M. Wirsing: Abstrakte Datentypen: Die algebraische Definition von Rechenstrukturen. *Informatik Spektrum* 5, 107–119 (1982).

[BBGGG 85]   M. Bidoit, B. Biebow, M.-C. Gaudel, C. Gresse, G. Guiho: Exception handling: formal specification and systematic program construction. *IEEE Trans. on Software Engineering* SE-11(3), 242–252 (1985).

[BBGN 90]   M. Breu, M. Broy, T. Grünler, F. Nickl: Semantics of PA^{nn}dA-S. In: PROgram development by SPECification and TRAnsformation. Vol. II: Language Family (B. Krieg-Brückner, ed.). PROSPECTRA Report M.1.1.S3-R-56.2, Universität Bremen (1990). Springer LNCS, to appear.

[BBTW 81]   J.A. Bergstra, M. Broy, J.V. Tucker, M. Wirsing: On the power of algebraic specifications. *Proc. 1981 Symp. on Mathematical Foundations of Computer Science.* Springer LNCS 118, 193–204 (1981).

[BC 85]   M. Bidoit, C. Choppy: ASSPEGIQUE: an integrated environment for algebraic specifications. *Proc. Joint Conf. on Theory and Practice of Software Development,* Berlin. Springer LNCS 186, 246–260 (1985).

[BC 87]   V. Breazu-Tannen, T. Coquand: Extensional models of polymorphism. *Proc. Joint Conf. on Theory and Practice of Software Development,* Pisa. Springer LNCS 250, 291–307 (1987).

[BCFG 86]   L. Bougé, N. Choquet, L. Fribourg, M.-C. Gaudel: Test sets generation from algebraic specifications using logic programming. *Journal of Systems and Software* 6(4), 343–360 (1986).

[BCM 88]   E. Battiston, F. De Cindio, G. Mauri: OBJSA nets: a class of high-level nets having abstract data types as domains. *Advances in Petri Nets '88.* Springer LNCS 340 (1988).

[BCV 84]   M. Bidoit, C. Choppy, F. Voisin: The ASSPEGIQUE specification environment: motivations and design. *Recent Trends in Data Type Specification, Proc. 3rd Workshop on Theory and Applications of Abstract Data Types*, Bremen. Springer IFB 116, 54–72 (1985).

[BD 86a]   L. Bachmair, N. Dershowitz: Critical pair criteria for the Knuth-Bendix completion procedure. Technical Report, Univ. of Illinois at Urbana-Champaign (1986).

[BD 86b]   L. Bachmair, N. Dershowitz: Commutation, transformation and termination. *Proc. 8th Conf. on Automated Deduction*, Oxford. Springer LNCS 230 (1986).

[BDH 86]   L. Bachmair, N. Dershowitz, J. Hsiang: Orderings for equational proofs. *Proc. IEEE Symp. on Logic in Computer Science*, Boston, 346–357 (1986).

[BDJ 78]   D. Brand, J.A. Darringer, W.H. Joyner: Completeness of conditional reductions. Report RC-7404, IBM T.J. Watson Research Center, Yorktown Heights (1978).

[BDPPW 79]   M. Broy, W. Dosch, H. Partsch, P. Pepper, M. Wirsing: Existential quantifiers in abstract data types. *Proc. 6th Intl. Colloq. on Automata, Languages and Programming*. Springer LNCS 71, 73–87 (1979).

[BEGKPS 87]   H.P. Barendregt, M.C.J.D. van Eekelen, J.R.W. Glauert, J.R. Kennaway, M.J. Plasmeijer, M.R. Sleep: Term graph rewriting. Internal report 87, University of Nijmegen (1987).

[BEP 87]   E.K. Blum, H. Ehrig, F. Parisi-Presicce: Algebraic specification of modules and their basic interconnections. *Journal of Computer and System Sciences* 34, 293–339 (1987).

[BG 77]   R.M. Burstall, J.A. Goguen: Putting theories together to make specifications. *Proc. 5th Intl. Joint Conf. on Artificial Intelligence*, Cambridge, Massachusetts, 1045–1058 (1977).

[BG 80]   R.M. Burstall, J.A. Goguen: The semantics of CLEAR, a specification language. *Proc. Advanced Course on Abstract Software Specifications*, Copenhagen. Springer LNCS 86, 292–332 (1980).

[BG 83]   M. Bidoit, M.-C. Gaudel: Spécification des cas d'exceptions dans les types abstraits algébriques: problèmes et perspectives. Report 146, LRI, Université de Paris-Sud, Orsay (1983).

[BG 89]   V. Breazu-Tannen, J. Gallier: Polymorphic rewriting conserves algebraic strong normalization and confluence. *Proc. 16th Intl. Colloq. on Automata, Languages and Programming*. Springer LNCS 372, 137–150 (1989).

[BG 90a]   L. Bachmair, H. Ganzinger: On restrictions of ordered paramodulation with simplification. *Proc. 10th Conf. on Automated Deduction*. Springer LNCS (1990), to appear.

64

[BG 90b]   L. Bachmair, H. Ganzinger: Completion of first-order clauses with equality by strict superposition. *Proc. 2nd Intl. Workshop on Conditional and Typed Rewriting*, Montreal. Springer LNCS (1990), to appear.

[BGM 89]   M. Bidoit, M.-C. Gaudel, A. Mauboussin: How to make algebraic specifications more understandable? An experiment with the PLUSS specification language. *Science of Computer Programming* 12, 1–38 (1989).

[BH 84]   W. Bibel, K.M. Hoernig: LOPS — a system based on a strategical approach to program synthesis. In: *Automatic Program Construction Techniques* (A.W. Biermann, G. Guiho, Y. Kodratoff eds.). Macmillan, 69–91 (1984).

[BH 85]   B. Biebow, J. Hagelstein: Algebraic specification of synchronisation and errors: a telephonic example. *Proc. Joint Conf. on Theory and Practice of Software Development*, Berlin. Springer LNCS 186, 294–308 (1985).

[BHK 89]   J.A. Bergstra, J. Heering, R. Klint (eds.): *Algebraic Specification*. Addison-Wesley (1989).

[BHK 90]   J.A. Bergstra, J. Heering, R. Klint: Module algebra. *Journal of the Assoc. for Computing Machinery* 37(2), 335–372 (1990).

[BHR 84]   S.D. Brookes, C.A.R. Hoare, A.W. Roscoe: A theory of communicating sequential processes. *Journal of the Assoc. for Computing Machinery* 31(3), 560–599 (1984).

[BK 81]   J.A. Bergstra, J.W. Klop: Initial algebra specifications for parameterized data types. Technical Report IW 186, Mathematical Centrum, Dept. of Computer Science, Amsterdam (1981).

[BK 82]   J.A. Bergstra, J.W. Klop: Conditional rewrite rules: confluence and termination. Technical Report, Mathematical Centrum, Dept. of Computer Science, Amsterdam (1982).

[BK 86]   J.A. Bergstra, J.W. Klop: Algebra of communicating processes. *Proc. CWI Symp. Math. and Computer Science*. North Holland (1986).

[BL 87]   F. Bellegarde, P. Lescanne: Transformation orderings. *Proc. Joint Conf. on Theory and Practice of Software Development*, Pisa. Springer LNCS 249 (1987).

[BL 88]   R.M. Burstall, B. Lampson: A kernel language for abstract data types and modules. *Information and Computation* 76, 278–346 (1988).

[BLMO 86]   R. Butler, E. Lusk, W. McCune, R. Overbeek: Paths to high-performance theorem proving. *Proc. 8th Conf. on Automated Deduction*, Oxford. Springer LNCS 230, 588–597 (1986).

[BM 79]   R.S. Boyer, J.S. Moore: *A Computational Logic*. Academic Press (1979).

[BM 88]   R.S. Boyer, J.S. Moore: *A Computational Logic Handbook*. Academic Press (1988).

[BMPW 86]   M. Broy, B. Möller, P. Pepper, M. Wirsing: Algebraic implementations preserve program correctness. *Science of Computer Programming* 7, 35–53 (1986).

[BP 81]   M. Broy, P. Pepper: Program development as a formal activity. *IEEE Trans. on Software Engineering* SE-7(1), 14–22 (1981).

[BP 82]   M. Broy, P. Pepper: Combining algebraic and algorithmic reasoning: an approach to the Schorr-Waite algorithm. *ACM Trans. on Programming Languages and Systems* 4(3), 362–381 (1982).

[BP 83]   M. Broy, P. Pepper: On the coherence of programming language and programming methodology. *Proc. IFIP TC2 Working Conf. on Programming Languages and System Design*, Dresden. North Holland, 41–53 (1983).

[BP 85]   L. Bachmair, D.A. Plaisted: Termination orderings for associative-commutative rewriting systems. *Journal of Symbolic Computation* (1985).

[BPPW 77]   F.L. Bauer, H. Partsch, P. Pepper, H. Wössner: Techniques for program development. *Software Engineering Techniques. Infotech State of the Art Report 34*. Infotech International, 25–50 (1977).

[BPPW 78]   F.L. Bauer, H. Partsch, P. Pepper, H. Wössner: A transformational approach to programming. *Proc. 3rd Symp. on Programming*, Paris. Dunod 248–262 (1978).

[BPPW 80]   M. Broy, H. Partsch, P. Pepper, M. Wirsing: Semantic relations in programming languages. *Proc. IFIP Congress 1980*, Melbourne. North-Holland, 101–106 (1980).

[BPW 80]   M. Broy, P. Pepper, M. Wirsing: On relations between programs. *Proc. 4th Symp. on Programming*, Paris. Springer LNCS 83, 59–78 (1980).

[BPW 81]   M. Broy, P. Pepper, M. Wirsing: Programming in a wide-spectrum language. In: *Algorithmic languages* (J.W. de Bakker and J.C. von Vliet, eds.). North Holland, 73–114 (1981).

[BPW 84]   M. Broy, C. Pair, M. Wirsing: A systematic study of models of abstract data types. *Theoretical Computer Science* 33, 139–174 (1984).

[BPW 87]   M. Broy, P. Pepper, M. Wirsing: On the algebraic definition of programming languages. *ACM Trans. on Programming Languages and Systems* 9, 54–99 (1987).

[BR 88]   W. Bousdira, J.L. Rémy: Hierarchical contextual rewriting with several levels. *Proc. 5th Symp. on Theoretical Aspects of Computer Science*. Springer LNCS 294, 193–206 (1988).

66

[BT 83]   J.A. Bergstra, J.V. Tucker: Initial and final algebra semantics: two charac-
            terization theorems. *SIAM Journal on Computing* 12(2), 366–387 (1983).

[BT 87]   J.A. Bergstra, J.V. Tucker: Algebraic specifications of computable and
            semicomputable data types. *Theoretical Computer Science* 50, 137–181
            (1987).

[BV 87]   C. Beierle, A. Voß: Viewing implementations as an institution. *Proc.
            Summer Conf. on Category Theory and Computer Science*, Edinburgh.
            Springer LNCS 283, 196–218 (1987).

[BW 80]   M. Broy, M. Wirsing: Programming languages as abstract data types.
            Proc. 1980 Colloq. on Trees in Algebra and Programming, Lille, 160–177
            (1980).

[BW 81]   M. Broy, M. Wirsing: On the algebraic specification of nondeterminis-
            tic programming languages. *Proc. 1981 Colloq. on Trees in Algebra and
            Programming*, Genoa. Springer LNCS 112 (1981).

[BW 82a]   M. Broy, M. Wirsing: Partial abstract data types. *Acta Informatica* 18(1),
            47–64 (1982).

[BW 82b]   F.L. Bauer, H. Wössner: *Algorithmic Language and Program Develop-
            ment*. Springer (1982).

[BW 83a]   M. Broy, M. Wirsing: Algebraic definition of a functional programming
            language and its semantic models. *RAIRO Informatique Théorique* 17,
            137–161 (1983).

[BW 83b]   M. Broy, M. Wirsing: On the algebraic specification of finitary infinite
            communicating sequential processes. *Proc. IFIP TC2 Working Conf. on
            the Formal Description of Programming Concepts II*, Garmisch. North
            Holland (1983).

[BW 83c]   M. Broy, M. Wirsing: Generalized heterogeneous algebras and partial in-
            terpretations. *Proc. 1983 Colloq. on Trees in Algebra and Programming*,
            L'Aquila. Springer LNCS 159, 1–34 (1983).

[BW 85]   D.M. Berry, J.M. Wing: Specifying and prototyping: some thoughts on
            why they are successful. *Proc. Joint Conf. on Theory and Practice of
            Software Development*, Berlin. Springer LNCS 186 (1985).

[BW 88a]   F.L. Bauer, M. Wirsing: Crypt-equivalent algebraic specifications. *Acta
            Informatica* 25(2), 111–153 (1988).

[BW 88b]   R. Bird, P. Wadler: *Introduction to Functional Programming*. Prentice-
            Hall (1988).

[BZ 89]   R. Breu, E. Zucca: An algebraic compositional semantics of an object-
            oriented notation with concurrency. *Proc. 9th Conf. on Foundations of
            Software Technology and Theoretical Computer Science*. Springer LNCS
            405 (1989).

[Cap 87]   F. Capy: ASSPEGIQUE: un environnement d'exceptions ... Une
            sémantique opérationnelle des E,R-algèbres, formalisme prenant en
            compte les exceptions. Un environnement intégré de spécification
            algébrique: ASSPEGIQUE. Thèse de 3eme cycle, Université de Paris-Sud,
            Orsay (1987).

[Cla 89]   I. Claßen: Revised ACT ONE: categorical constructions for an algebraic
            specification language. *Proc Workshop on Categorical Methods in Com-
            puter Science with Aspects from Topology.* Springer LNCS 393, 124–141
            (1989).

[Cho 86]   M.-A. Choquer: Specification of the evaluation tool: leftmost-outermost
            reduction strategy in the equational case. METEOR report, LRI, Univer-
            sité de Paris-Sud, Orsay (1986).

[Cho 87]   C. Choppy: Formal specification, prototyping and integration tests. *Proc.
            European Software Engineering Conference*, Strasbourg, 185–192, (1987).

[Clé 89]   S. Clérici. Un lenguaje para el diseño y validación de especificaciones al-
            gebraicas. Ph.D. Thesis, Universitat Politècnica de Catalunya, Barcelona
            (1989).

[Col 84]   A. Colmerauer: Equations and inequations on finite and infinite trees.
            Proc. Intl. Conf on 5th Generation Computing Systems, Tokyo, 85–99,
            (1984).

[Col 85]   A. Colmerauer: Introduction à Prolog III. Groupe Intelligence Artificielle,
            Université d'Aix-Marseille II (1985).

[Com 85]   *IEEE Computer* 18(4) (1985).

[Com 88]   H. Comon: Unification et disunification. Théories et applications, Thèse
            de l'Institut Polytechnique de Grenoble (1988).

[Cox 86]   B.J. Cox: *Object-Oriented Programming: An Evolutionary Approach.*
            Addison-Wesley (1986).

[CD 83]   R.J. Cunningham, A.J.J. Dick: Rewrite systems on a lattice of types.
            Technical Report, Imperial College (1983).

[CG 85]   S. Ceri, G. Gottlob: Translating SQL into relational algebra: optimiza-
            tion, semantics, and equivalence of SQL queries. *IEEE Trans. on Software
            Engineering* SE-11 (1985).

[CH 85]   T. Coquand, G. Huet: Constructions: a higher-order proof system for
            mechanizing mathematics. *Proc. 1985 European Conf. on Computer Al-
            gebra*, Linz. Springer LNCS 204, 151–184 (1985).

[CIP 81]   F.L. Bauer, M. Broy, W. Dosch, T. Gnatz, B. Krieg-Brückner, A. Laut,
            M. Luckmann, T.A. Matzner, B. Möller, H. Partsch, P. Pepper, K. Samel-
            son, R. Steinbrüggen, M. Wirsing, H. Wössner: Programming in a wide

spectrum language: a collection of examples. *Science of Computer Programming* 1, 73–114 (1981).

[CIP 85]   F.L. Bauer, R. Berghammer, M. Broy, W. Dosch, F. Geiselbrechtinger, R. Gnatz, E. Hangel, W. Hesse, B. Krieg-Brückner, A. Laut, T. Matzner, B. Möller, F. Nickl, H. Partsch, P. Pepper, K. Samelson, M. Wirsing, H.Wössner: *The Munich Project CIP, Vol. 1: The Wide Spectrum Language CIP-L.* Springer LNCS 183 (1985).

[CIP 87]   F.L. Bauer, H. Ehler, R. Horsch, B. Möller, H. Partsch, O. Paukner, P. Pepper: *The Munich project CIP. Volume II: The Transformation System CIP-S.* Springer LNCS 292 (1987).

[CJ 85a]   C. Choppy, C. Johnen: PETRIREVE: Petri net transformations and proofs with rewriting systems. *Proc. 6th European Workshop on Applications and Theory of Petri Nets*, Helsinki (1985).

[CJ 85b]   C. Choppy, C. Johnen: PETRIREVE: proving Petri net properties with rewriting systems. *Proc. Conf. on Rewriting Techniques and Applications*, Dijon. Springer LNCS 202, 271–286 (1985).

[CL 73]   C.L. Chang, R.C. Lee: *Symbolic Logic and Mechanical Theorem Proving.* Academic Press (1973).

[CL 87]   A. Ben Cherifa, P. Lescanne: Termination of rewriting systems by polynomial interpretations and its implementation. *Science of Computer Programming* (1987).

[CL 89]   H. Comon, P. Lescanne: Equational problems and disunification. *Journal of Symbolic Computation* 3-4(7),371–426 (1989).

[CO 88]   S. Clérici, F. Orejas: GSBL: an algebraic specification language based on inheritance. *Proc. 1988 European Conf. on Object Oriented Programming*, Oslo. Springer LNCS 322, 78–92 (1988).

[CW 85]   L. Cardelli, P. Wegner: On understanding types, data abstraction, and polymorphism. *Computing Surveys* 17, 471–522 (1985).

[Der 82]   N. Dershowitz: Orderings for term-rewriting systems. *Theoretical Computer Science* (1982).

[Der 83]   N. Dershowitz: Applications of the Knuth-Bendix completion procedure. Aerospace Report ATR-83(8478)-2, El Segundo, California (1983).

[Der 85]   N. Dershowitz: Synthesis by completion. *Proc. 9th Intl. Joint Conf. on Artificial Intelligence*, Los Angeles, 208–214 (1985).

[Der 87]   N. Dershowitz: Termination of rewriting. *Journal of Symbolic Computation* (1987).

[Der 89]   N. Dershowitz: Completion and its applications. *Proc. Colloq. on Resolution of Equations in Algebraic Structures*, Austin. Academic Press (1989).

69

[Des 83]   J. Despeyroux-Savonitto: An algebraic specification of a Pascal compiler. *SIGPLAN Notices* 18(12), 34–48 (1983).

[Die 88]   N. van Diepen: Implementation of modular algebraic specifications. *Proc. 1988 European Symp. on Programming.* Springer LNCS 300, 64–78 (1988).

[Dro 83]   K. Drosten: Towards executable specifications using conditional axioms. Report 83-01, Technische Universität Braunschweig (1983).

[DJ 89]   N. Dershowitz, J.P. Jouannaud: Rewriting systems. *Handbook of Theoretical Computer Science.* North Holland, to appear.

[DMN 70]   O.-J. Dahl, B. Myrhaug, K. Nygaard: Simula 67 common base language. Report S-22, Norwegian Computing Center, Oslo (1970); revised edition 1984.

[DMT 88]   N. Dershowitz, L. Marcus, A. Tarlecki: Existence, uniqueness, and construction of rewrite systems. *SIAM Journal on Computing* 17(4), 629–639 (1988).

[DMW 82]   W. Dosch, G. Mascari, M. Wirsing: On the algebraic specification of databases. *Proc. 8th Conf. on Very Large Data Bases* (1982).

[DP 89]   N. van Diepen, H. Partsch: Some aspects of formalizing informal requirements. *Proc. METEOR Workshop*, Mierlo (1989).

[Ehl 85]   H. Ehler: Making formal specifications readable. Report TUM-I8527, Technische Universität München (1985).

[Ehr 81]   H. Ehrig: Algebraic theory of parameterized specifications with requirements. *Proc. 1981 Colloq. on Trees in Algebra and Programming.* Springer LNCS 112, 1–24 (1981).

[Ehr 82]   H.-D. Ehrich: On the theory of specification, implementation and parameterization of abstract data types. *Journal of the Assoc. for Computing Machinery* 29, 206–227 (1982).

[Ehr 84]   H. Ehrig: Combining initial and loose algebraic specification methods including compositionality and modules. *Proc. Workshop on Formal Software Development: Combining Specification Methods*, Nyborg (1984).

[Eis 86]   N. Eisinger: What you always wanted to know about clause graph resolution. *Proc. 8th Conf. on Automated Deduction*, Oxford. Springer LNCS 230, 316–336 (1986).

[EF 81]   H. Ehrig, W. Fey: Methodology for the specification of software system: from formal requirements to algebraic design specifications. *GI — 11. Jahrestagung.* Springer IFB 50, 255–269 (1981).

[EF 83]   H. Ehrig, W. Fey: Algebraic concepts applied to software development using parameterized specifications with requirements. Technical Report 83-13, Technische Universität Berlin (1983).

[EFH 83a]   H. Ehrig, W. Fey, H. Hansen: ACT ONE: an algebraic specification language with two levels of semantics. Technical Report 83-03, Technische Universität Berlin (1983).

[EFH 83b]   H. Ehrig, W. Fey, K.P. Hasler: Algebraische Spezifikationen: Konzepte und Sprachen für die Software-Entwicklung. Tagungsband "10 Jahre Informatik an der Universität Dortmund", (1983).

[EFH 85]   H. Ehrig, W. Fey, H. Hansen: Towards abstract user interfaces for formal system specifications. *Recent Trends in Data Type Specification, Proc. 3rd Workshop on Theory and Applications of Abstract Data Types*, Bremen. Springer IFB 116 (1985).

[EFHJL 89]   H. Ehrig, W. Fey, H. Hansen, D. Jacobs, M. Löwe: Algebraic concepts for the evolution of module families. *Proc. Intl. Conf. on Algebraic Methodology and Software Technology*, Iowa City, 85–88 (1989).

[EFHLJ 89]   H. Ehrig, W. Fey, H. Hansen, M. Löwe, D. Jacobs: Algebraic software development concepts for module and configuration families. *Proc. 9th Conf. on Foundations of Software Technology and Theoretical Computer Science*. Springer LNCS 405, 181–192 (1989).

[EFHLJLP 89]   H. Ehrig, W. Fey, H. Hansen, M. Löwe, D. Jacobs, A. Langen, F. Parisi-Presicce: Algebraic specification of modules and configuration families. *Journal Inf. Process. Cybern. EIK* 25(5/6), 205–232 (1989).

[EFHLP 87]   H. Ehrig, W. Fey, H. Hansen, M. Löwe, F. Parisi-Presicce: Algebraic theory of modular specification development. Technical Report 87-06, Technische Universität Berlin (1987).

[EFP 86]   H. Ehrig, W. Fey, F. Parisi-Presicce: Distributive laws for composition and union of module specification for software systems. *Proc. IFIP TC2 Working Conference on Program Specification and Transformation*, Bad Tölz. North-Holland, 293–312 (1986).

[EFPB 86]   H. Ehrig, W. Fey, F. Parisi-Presicce, E.K. Blum: Algebraic theory of module specifications with constraints. *Proc. 1986 Symp. on Mathematical Foundations of Computer Science*, Bratislava. Springer LNCS 233, 59–77 (1986).

[EGL 89]   H.-D. Ehrich, M. Gogolla, U.W. Lipeck: *Algebraische Spezifikation abstrakter Datentypen*. Teubner-Verlag (1989).

[EK 83]   H. Ehrig, H.-J. Kreowski: Compatibility of parameter passing and implementation of parameterized data types. *Theoretical Computer Science* 27(3), 255–286 (1983).

[EKMP 82]   H. Ehrig, H.-J. Kreowski, B. Mahr, P. Padawitz: Algebraic implementation of abstract data types. *Theoretical Computer Science* 20, 209–263 (1982).

[EKP 78]   H. Ehrig, H.-J. Kreowski, P. Padawitz: Stepwise specification and implementation of abstract data types. *Proc. 5th Intl. Colloq. on Automata, Languages and Programming*, Udine. Springer LNCS 62, 205–226 (1978).

[EKP 79]   H. Ehrig, H.-J. Kreowski, P. Padawitz: Algebraic implementation of abstract data types: an announcement. *SIGACT News* 11(2), 25–29 (1979).

[EKP 80]   H. Ehrig, H.-J. Kreowski, P. Padawitz: Completeness in algebraic specification. *EATCS Bulletin* 11, 2–9 (1980).

[EKTWW 84] H. Ehrig, H.-J. Kreowski, J. Thatcher, E. Wagner, J. Wright: Parameter passing in algebraic specification languages. *Theoretical Computer Science* 28, 45–81 (1984).

[EKW 78]   H. Ehrig, H.-J. Kreowski, H. Weber: Algebraic specification schemes for data base systems. *Proc. 4th Conf. on Very Large Data Bases*, Berlin (1978).

[EKW 79]   H. Ehrig, H.-J. Kreowski, H. Weber: Neue Aspekte algebraischer Spezifikationsschemata für Datenbanksysteme. *Proc. Workshop Formale Modelle für Informationssysteme*. Springer IFB 21, 181–198 (1979).

[EM 81]   H. Ehrig, B. Mahr: Complexity of algebraic implementations for abstract data types. *Journal of Computer and System Sciences* 23(2), 223–253 (1981).

[EM 85]   H. Ehrig, B. Mahr: *Fundamentals of Algebraic Specification 1. Equations and Initial Semantics*. EATCS Monographs on Theoretical Computer Science, Vol. 6. Springer (1985).

[EM 90]   H. Ehrig, B. Mahr: *Fundamentals of Algebraic Specification 2. Module Specifications and Constraints*. EATCS Monographs on Theoretical Computer Science, Vol. 21. Springer (1990).

[EPBRDG 87] H. Ehrig, F. Parisi-Presicce, P. Boehm, C. Rieckhoff, C. Dimitrovici, M. Große-Rhode: Combining data type and recursive process specifications using projection algebras. *Theoretical Computer Science*, to appear.

[EPBRDG 88] H. Ehrig, F. Parisi-Presicce, P. Boehm, C. Rieckhoff, C. Dimitrovici, M. Große-Rhode: Algebraic data type and process specifications based on projection spaces. *Recent Trends in Data Type Specification, Selected Papers from the 5th Workshop on Specification of Abstract Data Types*, Gullane, Scotland. Springer LNCS 332, 23–43 (1988).

[EPE 81]   G. Engels, V. Pletat, H. Ehrich: Handling errors and exceptions in the algebraic specification of data types. *Osnabrücker Schriften zur Mathematik* (1981).

[ER 76]   H. Ehrig, B.K. Rosen: Commutativity of independent transformations on complex objects. Report RC-6251, IBM T.J. Watson Research Center, Yorktown Heights (1976).

72

[ESS 89a]   H.-D. Ehrich, A. Sernadas, C. Sernadas: From data types to object types. *Journal Inf. Process. Cybern. EIK*, to appear.

[ESS 89b]   H.-D. Ehrich, A. Sernadas, C. Sernadas: Objects, object types, and object identification. *Proc Workshop on Categorical Methods in Computer Science with Aspects from Topology*. Springer LNCS 393 (1989).

[ETLZ 84]   H. Ehrig, J.W. Thatcher, P. Lucas, S.N. Zilles: Denotational and initial algebra semantics of the algebraic specification language LOOK. Technical Report 84-22, Technische Universität Berlin (1984).

[EW 85]   H. Ehrig, H. Weber: Algebraic specification of modules. *Proc. IFIP Working Conf. on Formal Models in Programming*. North-Holland, 231–258 (1985).

[EW 86]   H. Ehrig, H. Weber: Programming in the large with algebraic module specifications. *Proc. IFIP Congress 1986*. North-Holland, 675–684 (1986).

[EY 87]   M.H. van Emden, K. Yukawa: Logic programming with equations. *Journal of Logic Programming* (1987).

[Fag 84]   F. Fages: Associative-commutative unification. *Proc. 7th Conf. on Automated Deduction*. Springer LNCS 170, 194–208 (1984).

[Far 89]   J. Farrés-Casals: Proving correctness of constructor implementations. *Proc. 1989 Symp. on Mathematical Foundations of Computer Science*. Springer LNCS 379, 225–235 (1989).

[Fay 79]   M. Fay: First order unification in equational theories. *Proc. 4th Conf. on Automated Deduction*. Springer LNCS 87, 161–167 (1979).

[Fey 80]   W. Fey: Syntax, Semantic und Korrektheit eines algebraischen Spezifikationsschemas für ein Stücklisten-Datenbanksystem. Technical Report 80-12, Technische Universität Berlin (1980).

[Fey 86]   W. Fey: Introduction to algebraic specification in ACT TWO. Technical Report 86-13, Technische Universität Berlin (1986).

[Fey 88]   W. Fey: Pragmatics, Concepts, Syntax, Semantics, and Correctness Notions of ACT TWO: An Algebraic Module Specification and Interconnection Language. Ph.D. thesis; Technical Report 88-26, Technische Universität Berlin (1988).

[Fra 88a]   M. Franova: An implementation of program synthesis from formal specifications. *Proc. 8th European Conf. on Artificial Intelligence*. Pitman, 559–564 (1988).

[Fra 88b]   M. Franova: Fundamentals for a new methodology for inductive theorem proving: CM-construction of atomic formulae. *Proc. 8th European Conf. on Artificial Intelligence*. Pitman, 137–141 (1988).

[Fra 88c]   M. Franova: Fundamentals of a New Methodology for Program Synthesis from Formal Specifications: CM-construction of Atomic Formulae. Ph.D. thesis, Université de Paris-Sud, Orsay (1988).

[Fri 84]   L. Fribourg: Oriented equational clauses as a programming language. Report 84002, Laboratoires de Marcoussis (1984). Short version in: *Proc. 11th Intl. Colloq. on Automata, Languages and Programming.* Springer LNCS 172, 162–173 (1984).

[Fri 85]   L. Fribourg: SLOG: a logic programming language interpreter based on clausal superposition and rewriting. *Proc. 1985 IEEE Symp. on Logic Programming,* 172–184 (1985).

[Fri 86]   L. Fribourg: A strong restriction of the inductive completion procedure. *Proc. 13th Intl. Colloq. on Automata, Languages and Programming,* Rennes. Springer LNCS 226, 105–115 (1986).

[Fri 88]   L. Fribourg: Prolog with simplification. *Programming of Future Generation Computers,* North-Holland (1988).

[FD 85]   R. Forgaard, D. Detlefs: An incremental algorithm for proving termination of term rewriting sytems. *Proc. Conf. on Rewriting Techniques and Applications,* Dijon. Springer LNCS 202, 255–270 (1985).

[FGJM 85]   K. Futatsugi, J.A. Goguen, J.-P. Jouannaud, J. Meseguer: Principles of OBJ2. *Proc. 12th ACM Symp. on Principles of Programming Languages,* New Orleans, 52–66 (1985).

[FGMO 87]   K. Futatsugi, J. Goguen, J. Meseguer, K. Okada: Parameterized programming in OBJ2. *Proc. 9th IEEE Intl. Conf. on Software Engineering,* 50–61 (1987).

[FJKR 87]   L.M.G. Feijs, H.B.M. Jonkers, C.P.J. Koymans, G.R. Renardel de Lavalette: Formal definition of the design language COLD-K. METEOR Report t7/PRLE/7, Philips Research Lab., Eindhoven (1987).

[FJOKRR 87]   L.M.G. Feijs, H.B.M. Jonkers, J.H. Obbink, C.P.J. Koymans, G.R. Renardel de Lavalette, P.M. Rodenburg: A survey of the design language COLD. *Proc. ESPRIT Conf. '86: Results and Achievements.* North Holland, 631–644 (1987).

[FK 87]   J.H. Fasel, R.M. Keller (eds.): *Graph Reduction.* Springer LNCS 279 (1987).

[FS 88]   J. Fiadeiro, A. Sernadas: Structuring theories on consequence. *Recent Trends in Data Type Specification, Selected Papers from the 5th Workshop on Specification of Abstract Data Types,* Gullane, Scotland. Springer LNCS 332 (1988).

74

[FSS 88]   J. Fiadeiro, A. Sernadas, C. Sernadas: Knowledge bases as structured theories. *Proc. 8th Conf. on Foundations of Software Technology and Theoretical Computer Science.* Springer LNCS 338, 469–486 (1988).

[Gal 86]   J. H. Gallier: *Logic for Computer Science: Foundations of Automatic Theorem Proving.* Harper and Row (1986).

[Gan 83]   H. Ganzinger: Parameterized specifications: parameter passing and implementation with respect to observability. *ACM Trans. on Programming Languages and Systems* 5(3), 318–354 (1983).

[Gan 87a]   H. Ganzinger: Ground term confluence in parametric conditional equational specifications. *Proc. 4th Symp. on Theoretical Aspects of Computer Science*, Passau. Springer LNCS 247, 193–206 (1987).

[Gan 87b]   H. Ganzinger: A completion procedure for conditional equations. *Proc. Intl. Workshop on Conditional Term Rewriting*, Orsay. Springer LNCS 308 (1987); *Journal of Symbolic Computation*, to appear.

[Gan 88]   H. Ganzinger: Completion with history-dependent complexities for generated equations. *Recent Trends in Data Type Specification, Selected Papers from the 5th Workshop on Specification of Abstract Data Types*, Gullane, Scotland. Springer LNCS 332 (1988).

[Gan 89]   H. Ganzinger: Order-sorted completion: the many-sorted way. *Proc. Joint Conf. on Theory and Practice of Software Development*, Barcelona. Springer LNCS 351, 244–259 (1989); *Theoretical Computer Science*, to appear.

[Gau 84]   M.-C. Gaudel: A first introduction to PLUSS. Technical Report, LRI, Université de Paris-Sud, Orsay (1984).

[Gau 85]   M.-C. Gaudel: Towards structured algebraic specifications. *Esprit '85 Status Report.* North-Holland, 493–510 (1985).

[Ges 89]   A. Geser: A specification of the Intel 8085 microprocessor: a case study. *Algebraic Methods: Theory, Tools and Applications.* Springer LNCS 394, 347–401 (1989).

[Gna 86]   I. Gnaedig: Proving termination of associative rewriting systems by rewriting. Thèse de la Université de Nancy I (1986).

[Gog 78a]   J.A. Goguen: Abstract errors for abstract data types. *Proc. IFIP Working Conference on the Formal Description of Programming Concepts*, New Brunswick, New Jersey. North-Holland (1978).

[Gog 78b]   J.A. Goguen: Exceptions and error sorts, coercion and overloaded operators. Technical Report, SRI (1978).

[Gog 84a]   J.A. Goguen: Parameterized programming. *IEEE Trans. on Software Engineering* SE-10(5), 528–543 (1984).

[Gog 84b]   M. Gogolla: Partially ordered sorts in algebraic specifications. *Proc. 1984 Colloq. on Trees in Algebra and Programming*, Bordeaux. Cambridge Univ. Press, 139–153 (1984).

[Gog 85]   M. Gogolla: A final algebra semantics for errors and exceptions. *Recent Trends in Data Type Specification, Proc. 3rd Workshop on Theory and Applications of Abstract Data Types*, Bremen. Springer IFB 116, 89–103 (1985).

[Gog 86]   M. Gogolla: Über Partiell Geordnete Sortenmengen und deren Anwendung zur Fehlerbehandlung in Abstrakten Datentypen. Ph.D. thesis, Technische Universität Braunschweig (1986).

[Gog 87]   M. Gogolla: On parametric algebraic specifications with clean error handling. *Proc. Joint Conf. on Theory and Practice of Software Development*, Pisa. Springer LNCS 249, 81–95 (1987).

[Got 79]   S. Goto: Program synthesis from natural deduction proofs. *Proc. 6th Intl. Joint Conf. on Artificial Intelligence*, Tokyo, 339–341 (1979).

[Gri 87]   T.G. Griffin: An environment for formal systems. Report ECS-LFCS-87-34, Univ. of Edinburgh (1987).

[Gro 89]   M. Große-Rhode: Parameterized data type and process specifications using projection algebras. *Proc Workshop on Categorical Methods in Computer Science with Aspects from Topology*. Springer LNCS 393, 185–197 (1989).

[Gut 75]   J.V. Guttag: The Specification and Application to Programming of Abstract Data Types. Ph.D. thesis, Univ. of Toronto (1975).

[GB 80]   J.A. Goguen, R.M. Burstall: CAT, a system for the structured elaboration of correct programs from structured specifications. Technical report CSL-118, Computer Science Laboratory, SRI International (1980).

[GB 84]   J.A. Goguen, R.M. Burstall: Introducing institutions. *Proc. Logics of Programming Workshop*, Carnegie-Mellon. Springer LNCS 164, 221–256 (1984).

[GB 86]   J.A. Goguen, R.M. Burstall: A study in the foundations of programming methodology: specifications, institutions, charters and parchments. *Proc. Workshop on Category Theory and Computer Programming*, Guildford. Springer LNCS 240, 313–333 (1986).

[GDLE 84]   M. Gogolla, K. Drosten, U.W. Lipeck, H.-D. Ehrich: Algebraic and operational semantics of specifications allowing exceptions and errors. *Theoretical Computer Science* 34, 289–313 (1984).

[GE 83]   M. Gogolla, H.-D. Ehrich: Algebraic specifications with subsorts using declarations. *EATCS Bulletin* 21, 31–38 (1983).

[GG 89]   S.J. Garland, J.V. Guttag: An overview of LP, the Larch Prover. *Proc. 3rd Conf. on Rewriting Techniques and Applications*, Chapel Hill, North Carolina. Springer LNCS 355, 137–151 (1989).

[GGM 76]   V. Giarratana, F. Gimona, U. Montanari: Observability concepts in abstract data type specification. *Proc. 1976 Symp. on Mathematical Foundations of Computer Science*, Gdansk. Springer LNCS 45, 567–578 (1976).

[GH 78]   J.V. Guttag, J.J. Horning: The algebraic specification of abstract data types. *Acta Informatica* 10, 27–52 (1978).

[GH 85]   A. Geser, H. Hußmann: Rapid prototyping for algebraic specifications — examples for the use of the RAP system. Report MIP-8517, Universität Passau (1985). Revised version 1987.

[GH 86a]   A. Geser, H. Hußmann: Experiences with the RAP system — a specification interpreter combining term rewriting and resolution. *Proc. 1986 European Symp. on Programming.* Springer LNCS 213, 339–350 (1986).

[GH 86b]   M.J.C. Gordon, J.M.J. Herbert: Formal hardware verification methodology and its application to a network interface chip. *IEE Proceedings* 133, 255–269 (1986).

[GH 86c]   J.V. Guttag, J.J. Horning: Report on the Larch shared language. *Science of Computer Programming* 6(2), 103–134 (1986).

[GHM 76]   J.V. Guttag, E. Horowitz, D.R. Musser: Abstract data types and software validation. Research Report ISI/RR-76-48, University of Southern California (1976).

[GHM 78]   J.V. Guttag, E. Horowitz, D.R. Musser: The design of data type specifications. In: *Current Trends in Programming Methodology, Vol. 4: Data Structuring* (R.T. Yeh, ed.). Prentice-Hall, 60–79 (1978).

[GHM 87]   A. Geser, H. Hußmann, A. Mueck: A compiler for a class of conditional rewrite systems. *Proc. Intl. Workshop on Conditional Term Rewriting*, Orsay. Springer LNCS 308, 84–90 (1987).

[GHW 82]   J. V. Guttag, J.J. Horning, J.M. Wing: Some notes on putting formal specifications to productive use. *Science of Computer Programming* 2, 53–68 (1982).

[GJ 71]   J.H. Griesmer, R.D. Jenks: SCRATCHPAD/1 — an interactive facility for symbolic mathematics. *Proc. 2nd ACM Symp. on Symbolic and Algebraic Manipulation*, New York (1971).

[GJM 85]   J.A. Goguen, J.P. Jouannaud, J. Meseguer: Operational semantics of order-sorted algebra. *Proc. 12th Intl. Colloq. on Automata, Languages and Programming*, Nafplion. Springer LNCS 194, 221–231 (1985).

[GKK 88]   I. Gnaedig, C. Kirchner, H. Kirchner: Equational completion in order-sorted algebras. *Proc. 1988 Colloq. on Trees in Algebra and Programming*, Nancy. Springer LNCS 299 (1988).

[GL 86]   I. Gnaedig, P. Lescanne: Proving termination of associative rewriting systems by rewriting. *Proc. 8th Conf. on Automated Deduction*, Oxford. Springer LNCS 230 (1986).

[GM 82]   J.A. Goguen, J. Meseguer: Universal realization, persistent interconnection and implementation of abstract modules. *Proc. 9th Intl. Colloq. on Automata, Languages and Programming*, Aarhus. Springer LNCS 140, 265–281 (1982).

[GM 83]   J.A. Goguen, J. Meseguer: Order-sorted algebra I: partial and overloaded operations, errors and inheritance. Technical Report, SRI International, Computer Science Lab, to appear.

[GM 86]   J.A. Goguen, J. Meseguer: EQLOG: equality, types and generic modules for logic programming. In: *Logic Programming. Functions, relations and equations* (D. DeGroot and G. Lindstrom, eds.). Prentice Hall (1986).

[GM 87a]   J.A. Goguen, J. Meseguer: Order-sorted algebra solves the constructor-selector, multiple representation and coercion problem. *Proc. 2nd IEEE Symp. on Logic in Computer Science*, Cornell (1987).

[GM 87b]   J.A. Goguen, J. Meseguer: Unifying functional, object oriented and relational programming with logical semantics. In: *Research Directions in Object-Oriented Programming* (B. Shriver and P. Wegner, eds.). MIT Press, 417–477 (1987).

[GM 88a]   M.-C. Gaudel, B. Marre: Algebraic specifications and software testing: theory and application. Report 407, LRI, Université de Paris-Sud, Orsay (1988).

[GM 88b]   M.-C. Gaudel, T. Moineau: A theory of software reusability. *Proc. 1988 European Symp. on Programming*. Springer LNCS 300, 115–130 (1988).

[GMP 83]   J. Goguen, J. Meseguer, D. Plaisted: Programming with parameterized abstract objects in OBJ. *Theory and Practice of Software Technology*. North-Holland, 163–193 (1983).

[GMS 83]   F. Golshani, T. Maibaum, M. Sadler: A modal systems of algebras for database specification and query/update language support. *Proc. 9th Conf. on Very Large Data Bases* (1983).

[GMW 79]   M.J.C. Gordon, A.J.R.G. Milner, C.P. Wadsworth: *Edinburgh LCF*. Springer LNCS 78 (1979).

[GR 83]   A. Goldberg, D. Robson: *Smalltalk-80: The Language and Its Implementation*. Addison-Wesley (1983).

[GR 89]   A. Giovini, G. Reggio: Bisimulation models in algebraic specifications. *Proc. 3rd Italian Conf. of Theoretical Computer Science.* Worlds Scientific (1989).

[GS 90]   H. Ganzinger, R. Schäfers: System support for modular order-sorted Horn clause specifications. *Proc. 12th Int'l Conf. on Software Engineering*, Nice. IEEE Computer Society Press, 150–163 (1990).

[GTW 76]   J.A. Goguen, J.W. Thatcher, E.G. Wagner: An initial algebra approach to the specification, correctness and implementation of abstract data types. Report RC-6487, IBM T.J. Watson Research Center, Yorktown Heights (1976). Also in: *Current Trends in Programming Methodology, Vol. 4: Data Structuring* (R.T. Yeh, ed.). Prentice-Hall, 80–149 (1978).

[GW 88]   J.A. Goguen, T. Winkler: Introducing OBJ3. Research report SRI-CSL-88-9, SRI International (1988).

[Han 86]   H. Hansen: Von Algebraischen Spezifikationen zu Algebraischen Programmen. Ph.D. thesis; Technical report 87-2, Technische Universität Berlin (1983).

[Han 88]   H. Hansen: The ACT-system: experiences and future enhancements. *Recent Trends in Data Type Specification, Selected Papers from the 5th Workshop on Specification of Abstract Data Types*, Gullane, Scotland. Springer LNCS 332, 113–130 (1988).

[Hea 71]   A.C. Hearn: REDUCE 2 — A system and language for algebraic manipulation. *Proc. 2nd ACM Symp. on Symbolic and Algebraic Manipulation*, New York (1971).

[Hee 86]   J. Heering: Partial evaluation and ω-completeness of algebraic specifications. *Theoretical Computer Science* 43, 149–167 (1986).

[Hen 77]   L. Henkin: The logic of equality. *Mathematical Monthly* (1977).

[Hen 88]   R. Hennicker: Beobachtungsorientierte Spezifikationen. Ph.D. thesis, Universität Passau (1988).

[Hen 89]   R. Hennicker: Observational implementations. *Proc. 6th Symp. on Theoretical Aspects of Computer Science*, Paderborn. Springer LNCS 349 (1989).

[Her 30]   J. Herbrand: Recherches sur la théorie de la démonstration. *Travaux de la Soc. des Sciences et des Lettres de Varsovie*, Classe III (1930).

[Her 86]   A. Herold: Combination of unification algorithms. *Proc. 8th Conf. on Automated Deduction*, Oxford. Springer LNCS 230, 450–469 (1986).

[Her 87]   A. Herold: Combination of Unification Algorithms in Equational Theories. Ph.D. thesis, Universität Kaiserslautern (1987).

[Her 88]   M. Hermann: Chain properties of rule closures. Report 88-R-022, CRIN, Nancy (1988).

[Hes 88]   W.H. Hesselink: A mathematical approach to nondeterminism in data types. *ACM Trans. on Programming Languages and Systems* 10(1), 87–117 (1988).

[Hig 52]   G. Higman: Ordering by divisibility in abstract algebra. *Proc. London Math. Soc.* 3(2) (1952).

[Hoa 72]   C.A.R. Hoare: Proofs of correctness of data representations. *Acta Informatica* 1, 271–281 (1972).

[Hoa 85]   C.A.R. Hoare: *Communicating Sequential Processes.* Prentice-Hall (1985).

[Hsi 82]   J. Hsiang: Topics in automated theorem proving and program generation. Ph.D. thesis, Univ. of Illinois at Urbana-Champaign (1982).

[Hue 76]   G. Huet: Résolution d'équations dans les langages d'ordre 1, 2, ..., ω. Thèse d'Etat de l'Université de Paris (1976).

[Hue 81]   G. Huet: A complete proof of correctness of the Knuth-Bendix completion algorithm. *Journal of Computer and System Sciences* 23(1), 11–21 (1981).

[Hul 80]   J.M. Hullot: Canonical forms and unification. *Proc. 5th Conf. on Automated Deduction.* Springer LNCS 87, 318–334 (1980).

[Hus 85a]   H. Hußmann: Unification in conditional equational theories. *Proc. 1985 European Conf. on Computer Algebra*, Linz. Springer LNCS 204 (1985).

[Hus 85b]   H. Hußmann: Rapid prototyping for algebraic specifications: RAP system user's manual. Report MIP-8504, Universität Passau (1985).

[HHP 87]   R.W. Harper, F.A. Honsell, G.D. Plotkin: A framework for defining logics. *Proc. 2nd IEEE Symp. on Logic in Computer Science*, Cornell (1987).

[HK 83]   G. Hommel, D. Kroenig (eds.): *Requirements Engineering.* Springer IFB 74 (1983).

[HKP 88]   A. Habel, H.-J. Kreowski, D. Plump: Jungle evaluation. *Recent Trends in Data Type Specification, Selected Papers from the 5th Workshop on Specification of Abstract Data Types*, Gullane, Scotland. Springer LNCS 332 (1988).

[HL 88]   H. Hansen, M. Löwe: Modular algebraic specifications. *Proc. Intl. Workshop on Algebraic and Logic Programming*, Gaußig, 168–179 (1988).

[HL 89]   I. van Horebeek, J. Lewi: *Algebraic Specifications in Software Engineering.* Springer (1989).

[HMM 86]   R.W. Harper, D.B. MacQueen, R.G. Milner: Standard ML. Report ECS-LFCS-86-2, Univ. of Edinburgh (1986).

[HO 80]   G. Huet, D.C. Oppen: Equations and rewrite rules — a survey. In: *Formal Language Theory: Perspectives and Open Problems* (R. Book, ed.). Academic Press, 349–405 (1980).

[HP 86]   M. Hermann, I. Privara: On nontermination of Knuth-Bendix algorithm. *Proc. 13th Intl. Colloq. on Automata, Languages and Programming*, Rennes. Springer LNCS 226, 146–156 (1986).

[HP 88]   B. Hoffmann, D. Plump: Jungle evaluation for efficient term rewriting. *Proc. Intl. Workshop on Algebraic and Logic Programming*, Gaußig, (1988).

[HR 87]   J. Hsiang, M. Rusinowitch: On word problems in equational theories. *Proc. 14th Intl. Colloq. on Automata, Languages and Programming*. Springer LNCS 267 (1987).

[HR 89]   H. Hußman, C. Rank: Specification and prototyping of a compiler for a small applicative language. *Algebraic Methods: Theory, Tools and Applications*. Springer LNCS 394, 403–418 (1989).

[HST 89a] R. Harper, D. Sannella, A. Tarlecki: Structure and representation in LF. *Proc. 2nd IEEE Symp. on Logic in Computer Science*, Asilomar, 226–237 (1989).

[HST 89b] R. Harper, D. Sannella, A. Tarlecki: Logic representation. *Proc. 3rd Summer Conf. on Category Theory and Computer Science*, Manchester. Springer LNCS 389, 250–272 (1989).

[Jon 89]   H.B.M. Jonkers: An introduction to COLD-K. *Algebraic Methods: Theory, Tools and Applications*. Springer LNCS 394, 139–206 (1989).

[JHW 87]   S. Jähnichen, F.A. Hussain, M. Weber: Program development using a design calculus. *Proc. ESPRIT Conf. '86: Results and Achievements*. North Holland, 645–658 (1987).

[JK 84]   J.P. Jouannaud, H. Kirchner: Completion of a set of rules modulo a set of equations. *Proc. 11th ACM Symp. on Principles of Programming Languages*, Salt Lake City (1984).

[JK 86]   J.P. Jouannaud, E. Kounalis: Proof by induction in equational theories without constructors. *Proc. IEEE Symp. on Logic in Computer Science*, Boston, 358–366 (1986).

[JKK 83]   J.P. Jouannaud, C. Kirchner, H. Kirchner: Incremental construction of unification algorithms in equational theories. *Proc. 10th Intl. Colloq. on Automata, Languages and Programming*, Barcelona. Springer LNCS 154, 361–373 (1983).

[JLR 83]   J.P. Jouannaud, P. Lescanne, F. Reinig: Recursive decomposition order-
           ing. *Proc. IFIP TC2 Working Conf. on the Formal Description of Pro-
           gramming Concepts II*, Garmisch. North Holland, 331–346 (1983).

[JW 86]   J.P. Jouannaud, B. Waldman: Reductive conditional term rewriting sys-
           tems. *Proc. Working Conf. on the Formal Description of Programming
           Concepts*, Ebberup, Denmark (1986).

[Kap 81]   H. Kaphengst: What is computable for abstract data types? *Proc. 1981
           Colloq. on Foundations of Computation Theory*. Springer LNCS 117, 173–
           181 (1981).

[Kap 84]   S. Kaplan: Conditional rewrite rules. *Theoretical Computer Science* 33,
           175–193 (1984).

[Kap 85]   S. Kaplan: Fair conditional term rewriting systems: unification, termina-
           tion and confluence. *Recent Trends in Data Type Specification, Proc. 3rd
           Workshop on Theory and Applications of Abstract Data Types*, Bremen.
           Springer IFB 116 (1985).

[Kap 86]   S. Kaplan: Rewriting with a nondeterministic choice operator: from al-
           gebra to proofs. *Proc. 1986 European Symp. on Programming*. Springer
           LNCS 213, 351–374 (1986).

[Kap 87]   S. Kaplan: A compiler for conditional term rewriting systems. *Proc.
           2nd Conf. on Rewriting Techniques and Applications*, Bordeaux. Springer
           LNCS 256, 25–41 (1987).

[Ken 87]   J.R. Kennaway: On "On Graph Rewritings". *Theoretical Computer Sci-
           ence* 52, 37–58 (1987).

[Kir 85]   C. Kirchner: Méthodes et outils de conception systématique d'algorithmes
           d'unification dans les théories équationnelles. Thèse d'Etat de l'Université
           de Nancy I (1985).

[Kir 86]   C. Kirchner: Computing unification algorithms. *Proc. IEEE Symp. on
           Logic in Computer Science*, Boston, 206–216 (1986).

[Kir 87]   H. Kirchner: Schematization of infinite sets of rewrite rules. Application to
           the divergence of completion process. P.Lescanne, editor, *Proc. 2nd Conf.
           on Rewriting Techniques and Applications*, Bordeaux. Springer LNCS 256,
           180–191 (1987). *Theoretical Computer Science*, to appear.

[Kir 88]   C. Kirchner: Order-sorted equational unification. *Proc. 5th Intl. Conf. on
           Logic Programming*, Seattle. MIT Press (1988).

[Kir 89]   C. Kirchner: Methods and tools for equational unification. *Proc. Colloq. on
           Resolution of Equations in Algebraic Structures*, Austin. Academic Press
           (1989).

[Kla 83]   H.A. Klaeren: *Algebraische Spezifikation — eine Einführung*. Springer (1983).

[Kow 70]   R. Kowalski: Search strategies for theorem proving. *Machine Intelligence 5* (B. Meltzer and D. Michie, eds.). American Elsevier, 181–201 (1970).

[Kre 75]   G. Kreisel: Some uses of proof theory for finding computer programs. *Colloque International de Logique*, Clermont-Ferrand (1975).

[Kre 81a]   G. Kreisel: Neglected possibilities of processing assertions and proofs mechanically: choice of problems and data. In: *University-Level Computer-Assisted Instruction at Stanford, 1968–1980* (P. Suppes, ed.). Stanford University, 131–148 (1981).

[Kre 81b]   G. Kreisel: Extraction of bounds: interpreting some tricks of the trade. In: *University-Level Computer-Assisted Instruction at Stanford, 1968–1980* (P. Suppes, ed.). Stanford University, 149–164 (1981).

[Kre 81c]   H.-J. Kreowski: Algebraische Spezifikation von Softwaresystemen. *Proc. GACM-Konf. Software Engineering*. Teubner-Verlag, 46–74 (1981).

[Kre 85a]   G. Kreisel: Proof theory and the synthesis of programs: potential and limitations. *Proc. 1985 European Conf. on Computer Algebra*, Linz. Springer LNCS 204, 136–151 (1985).

[Kre 85b]   H.-J. Kreowski (ed.): *Recent Trends in Data Type Specification, Proc. 3rd Workshop on Theory and Applications of Abstract Data Types*, Bremen. Springer IFB 116 (1985).

[Kre 87]   H.-J. Kreowski: Partial algebras flow from algebraic specifications. *Proc. 14th Intl. Colloq. on Automata, Languages and Programming*. Springer LNCS 267, 521–530 (1987).

[Kri 86]   B. Krieg-Brückner: Systematic transformation of interface specifications. *Proc. IFIP TC2 Working Conference on Program Specification and Transformation*, Bad Tölz. North-Holland, 296–291 (1986).

[Kri 87]   B. Krieg-Brückner: Integration of program construction and verification: the PROSPECTRA methodology. *Proc. CRAI Intl. Spring Conf. on Innovative Software Factories and Ada*. Springer LNCS 275, 173–194 (1987).

[Kri 88a]   B. Krieg-Brückner: The PROSPECTRA methodology of program development. *Proc IFIP/IFAC Working Conf. on Hardware and Software for Real Time Process Control*, Warsaw (1988).

[Kri 88b]   B. Krieg-Brückner: Algebraic formalisation of program development by transformation. *Proc. 1988 European Symp. on Programming*. Springer LNCS 300 (1988).

83

[Kri 89a]   B. Krieg-Brückner (ed.): COMPASS, a COMPrehensive Algebraic approach to System Specification and development (ESPRIT Basic Research Working Group 3264): Objectives, State of the Art, References. Bericht Nr. 6/89, Universität Bremen (1989).

[Kri 89b]   B. Krieg-Brückner: Algebraic specification and functionals for transformational program and meta program development. *Proc. Joint Conf. on Theory and Practice of Software Development*, Barcelona. Springer LNCS 352, 36–59 (1989).

[Kri 90a]   B. Krieg-Brückner: COMPASS, a COMPrehensive Algebraic approach to System Specification and development, ESPRIT Basic Research Working Group 3264. *EATCS Bulletin* 40, 144–157 (1990).

[Kri 90b]   B. Krieg-Brückner: PROgram development by SPECification and TRAnsformation. *Technique et Science Informatiques.* Special Issue on Advanced Software Engineering in ESPRIT (1990).

[Kri 90c]   B. Krieg-Brückner (ed.): PROgram development by SPECification and TRAnsformation. Vol. I: Methodology; Vol. II: Language Family; Vol. III: System. PROSPECTRA Reports M.1.1.S3-R-55.2, -56.2, -57.2, Universität Bremen (1990). Springer LNCS, to appear.

[Kru 60]   J.B. Kruskal: Well-quasi-ordering, the Tree Theorem and Vazsonyi's Conjecture. *Trans. American Math. Soc.* 95, 210–225 (1960).

[KB 70]   D.E. Knuth, P.B. Bendix: Simple word problems in universal algebras. *Computational Problems in Abstract Algebra* (J. Leech, ed.). Pergamon Press, 263–297 (1970).

[KHGB 87]   B. Krieg-Brückner, B. Hoffmann, H. Ganzinger, M. Broy, R. Wilhelm, U. Möncke, B. Weisgerber, A. McGettrick, I.G. Campbell, G. Winterstein: PROgram development by SPECification and TRAnsformation. *Proc. ESPRIT Conf. '86: Results and Achievements.* North Holland, 301–312 (1987).

[KI 89]   H. Klaeren, K. Indermark: A new technique for compiling recursive function symbols. *Algebraic Methods: Theory, Tools and Applications.* Springer LNCS 394, 69–90 (1989).

[KKM 88]   C. Kirchner, H. Kirchner, J. Meseguer: Operational semantics of OBJ3. *Proc. 15th Intl. Colloq. on Automata, Languages and Programming*, Tampere. Springer LNCS 317, 287–301 (1988).

[KL 83]   B. Kutzler, F. Lichtenberger: *Bibliography on Abstract Data Types.* Springer IFB 68 (1983).

[KL 87]   C. Kirchner, P. Lescanne: Solving disequations. *Proc. 2nd IEEE Symp. on Logic in Computer Science*, Cornell, 347–352 (1987).

84

[KM 87]   D. Kapur, D.R. Musser: Proof by consistency. *Artificial Intelligence* 31(2), 125–157 (1987).

[KMS 85]   S. Khosla, T. Maibaum, M.Sadler: Database specification. *Proc. IFIP Working Conference on Database Semantics.* North Holland (1985).

[KQ 90]   H.-J. Kreowski, Z. Qian: Relation-sorted specifications with built-in co-ercers: basic notions and results. *Proc. 7th Symp. on Theoretical Aspects of Computer Science.* Springer LNCS 415, 165–175 (1990).

[KNS 85]   D. Kapur, P. Narendran, G. Sivakumar: A path ordering for proving termination of term rewrite systems. *Proc. Joint Conf. on Theory and Practice of Software Development,* Berlin. Springer LNCS 186, 173–187 (1985).

[KNZ 87]   D. Kapur, P. Narendran, H. Zhang: On sufficient completeness and related properties of term rewriting systems. *Acta Informatica* 24, 395–415 (1987).

[KP 83]   Y. Kodratoff, M. Picard: Complétion de systèmes de réécriture et synthèse de programmes à partir de leurs spécifications. Bigre No.35 (1983).

[KP 87]   S. Kaplan, A. Pnueli: Specification and implementation of concurrently accessed data structures: an abstract data type approach. *Proc. 4th Symp. on Theoretical Aspects of Computer Science,* Passau. Springer LNCS 247 (1987).

[KP 90]   B. Krieg-Brückner, D. Plump (eds.): COMPASS, a COMPrehensive Algebraic approach to System Specification and development (ESPRIT Basic Research Working Group 3264): First Interim Report. Universität Bremen (1990).

[KR 87]   E. Kounalis, M. Rusinowitch: On word problems in Horn logic. *Proc. Intl. Workshop on Conditional Term Rewriting,* Orsay. Springer LNCS 308 (1987).

[KR 89]   S. Kaplan, J.L. Rémy: Completion algoritms for conditional rewriting systems. *Proc. Colloq. on Resolution of Equations in Algebraic Structures,* Austin. Academic Press (1989).

[KS 88]   D. Kapur and M. Srivas: Computability and implementability issues in abstract data types. *Science of Computer Programming* 10, 33–63 (1988).

[Lan 79]   D.S. Lankford: On proving term rewriting systems are Noetherian. Technical Report, Louisiana Tech. University (1979).

[Lan 85]   A. Langen: PERSIST: Ein Programm zur Überprüfung syntaktischer, hinreichender Bedingungen für Persistenz parametrisierter algebraischer Spezifikationen. Technical Report 85-11, Technische Universität Berlin (1985).

[Les 82a]   P. Lescanne: Modèles non déterministes de types abstraits. *RAIRO Informatique Théorique* 16(3), 225–244 (1982).

[Les 82b]   P. Lescanne: Some properties of the decomposition ordering, a simplification ordering to prove termination of rewriting systems. *RAIRO Informatique Théorique* 16(4) 331–347, (1982).

[Les 83]   P. Lescanne: Computer experiments with the REVE term rewriting systems generator. *Proc. 10th ACM Symp. on Principles of Programming Languages* (1983).

[Les 84]   P. Lescanne: Uniform termination of term rewriting systems: recursive decomposition ordering with status. *Proc. 1984 Colloq. on Trees in Algebra and Programming*, Bordeaux. Cambridge Univ. Press (1984).

[Les 87]   P. Lescanne: Current trends in rewriting techniques and related problems. In: *Trends in Computer Algebra* (R. Janßen, ed.). Springer LNCS 296, 38–51 (1987).

[Les 89]   P. Lescanne: Completion procedures as transition rules + control. *Proc. Joint Conf. on Theory and Practice of Software Development*, Barcelona. Springer LNCS 351, 28–41 (1989).

[Lie 85]   H. Lieberman: Using protypal objects to implement shared behaviour in object oriented systems. *Proc. OOPSLA '85* (1985).

[Loe 81]   J. Loeckx: Algorithmic specifications of abstract data types. *Proc. 8th Intl. Colloq. on Automata, Languages and Programming*. Springer LNCS 115 (1981).

[Loe 88]   J. Loeckx: Algorithmic specifications: a constructive specification method for abstract data types. *ACM Trans. on Programming Languages and Systems* 9, 646–685 (1988).

[Löw 89]   M. Löwe: Implementing Algebraic Specifications by Graph Transformation Systems. *Journal Inf. Process. Cybern. EIK*, to appear.

[Lov 78]   D. Loveland: *Automatic Theorem Proving*. North-Holland (1978).

[LB 81]   N.A. Lynch, E.K. Blum: Relative complexity of algebras. *Math. Syst. Theory* 14, 193–214 (1981).

[LL 88]   T. Lehmann, J. Loeckx: The specification language of OBSCURE. *Recent Trends in Data Type Specification, Selected Papers from the 5th Workshop on Specification of Abstract Data Types*, Gullane, Scotland. Springer LNCS 332, 131–153 (1988).

[LLT 86]   A. Lazrek, P. Lescanne, J-J. Thiel: Proving inductive equalities, algorithms and implementation. Report 86-R-087, CRIN, Nancy (1986).

[LOTOS 84]   ISO: Information processing systems. Definition of the temporal ordering specification language LOTOS. TC97/16 N1987 (1984).

86

[LOTOS 88]   E. Brinksma (ed.): Information processing systems — open systems inter-connection. LOTOS: a formal description technique based on the tempo-ral ordering of observational behaviour, International Standard, ISO 8807 (1988).

[LP 82]   A. Laut, H. Partsch: Tuning algebraic specifications by type merging. *Proc. 5th Symp. on Programming*, Turin. Springer LNCS 137, 283–304 (1982).

[LS 76]   M. Livesey, J. Siekmann: Unification of bags and sets. Technical Report, Universität Karlsruhe (1976).

[Maj 79]   M.E. Majster: Data types, abstract data types and their specification problem. *Theoretical Computer Science* (1979).

[Mak 77]   G.S. Makanin: The problem of solvability of equations in a free semigroup. *Akad. Nauk. SSSR* 233(2) (1977).

[Mar 87]   U. Martin: How to choose the weights in the Knuth-Bendix ordering. *Proc. 2nd Conf. on Rewriting Techniques and Applications*, Bordeaux. Springer LNCS 256, 42–53 (1987).

[Mat 84]   Y. Matsumoto: Some experiences in promoting reusable software. *IEEE Trans. on Software Engineering* SE-10(5), 502–513 (1984).

[May 85]   B. Mayoh: Galleries and institutions. Report DAIMI PB-191, Aarhus University (1985).

[Mes 89]   J. Meseguer: General logics. *Proc. Logic Colloquium '87*, Granada. North Holland (1989).

[Mey 87a]   B. Meyer: Reusability: the case for object-oriented design. *IEEE Software* 4(2), 50–64 (1987).

[Mey 87b]   B. Meyer: Eiffel: programming for reusability and extendibility. *SIGPLAN Notices* 22(2), 85–94 (1987).

[Mil 80]   R. Milner: *A Calculus of Communicating Systems*. Springer LNCS 92 (1980).

[Mil 84]   A.J.R.G. Milner: The use of machines to assist in rigorous proof. *Proc. Trans. Royal Soc. London* A312, 411–422 (1984).

[Möl 85]   B. Möller: On the algebraic specification of infinite objects: ordered and continuous algebraic types. *Acta Informatica* 22, 537–578 (1985).

[Möl 86]   B. Möller: Algebraic specifications with higher-order operators. *Proc. IFIP TC2 Working Conference on Program Specification and Transformation*, Bad Tölz. North-Holland, 367–392 (1986).

[Möl 87]   B. Möller: Higher-Order Algebraic Specifications. Habilitationsschrift, Technische Universität München (1987).

[Mos 83]   P. Mosses: Abstract semantic algebras. *Proc. IFIP TC2 Working Conf. on the Formal Description of Programming Concepts II*, Garmisch. North Holland (1983).

[Mos 89]   P. Mosses: Unified algebras and modules. *Proc. 16th ACM Symp. on Principles of Programming Languages*, 329–343 (1989).

[MG 85]   J. Meseguer, J.A. Goguen: Initiality, induction and computability. In: *Algebraic Methods in Semantics* (M. Nivat and J. Reynolds, eds.). Cambridge Univ. Press, 459–540 (1985).

[MGS 89]   J. Meseguer, J.A. Goguen, G. Smolka: Order-sorted unification. *Proc. Colloq. on Resolution of Equations in Algebraic Structures*, Austin. Academic Press (1989).

[MM 82]   A. Martelli, U. Montanari: An efficient unification algorithm. *ACM Trans. on Programming Languages and Systems* 4, 258–282 (1982).

[MP 86]   B. Möller, H. Partsch: Formal specification of large-scale software: objectives, design decisions, and experiences in a concrete software project. *Proc. IFIP TC2 Working Conference on Program Specification and Transformation*, Bad Tölz. North-Holland, 491–515 (1986).

[MP 88]   C.-T. Mong, P.W. Purdom: Divergence in the completion of rewriting systems. *Proc. 9th Conf. on Automated Deduction*. Springer LNCS 310 (1988).

[MS 85]   D.B. MacQueen, D.T. Sannella: Completeness of proof systems for equational specifications. *IEEE Trans. on Software Engineering* SE-11(5), 454–461 (1985).

[MSS 89]   V. Manca, A. Salibra, G. Scollo: On the nature of TELLUS: a Typed Equational Logic Look over Uniform Specification. *Proc. 1989 Symp. on Mathematical Foundations of Computer Science*. Springer LNCS 379, 338–349 (1989).

[MSS 90]   V. Manca, A. Salibra, G. Scollo: Equational type logic. *Theoretical Computer Science*, to appear (1990).

[MTW 88]   B. Möller, A. Tarlecki, M. Wirsing: Algebraic specifications of reachable higher-order algebras. *Recent Trends in Data Type Specification, Selected Papers from the 5th Workshop on Specification of Abstract Data Types*, Gullane, Scotland. Springer LNCS 332, 154–169 (1988).

[MW 80]   Z. Manna, R. Waldinger: A deductive approach to program synthesis. *ACM Trans. on Programming Languages and Systems* 2(1), 90–121 (1980).

[Nav 87]   M.L. Navarro Gomez: Tecnicas de Reescritura par Especificaciones Condicionales. Ph.D. Thesis, Universitat Politècnica de Catalunya, Barcelona (1987).

88

[Nic 87]   F. Nickl: Algebraic Specification of Semantic Domain Constructions. Ph.D. thesis, Universität Passau (1987).

[Nip 86]   T. Nipkow: Non-deterministic data types: models and implementations. *Acta Informatica* 22, 629–661 (1986).

[Niv 80]   M. Nivat: Nondeterministic programs: an algebraic overview. *Proc. IFIP Congress 1980*, Melbourne. North-Holland (1980).

[Niv 87]   P. Nivela. Semantica de comportamiento para especificaciones algebraicas. Ph.D. Thesis, Universitat Politècnica de Catalunya, Barcelona (1987).

[NO 84]   M. Navarro, F. Orejas: On the equivalence of hierarchical and non-hierarchical rewriting in conditional term rewriting systems. *Proc. EUROSAM '84*, Cambridge. Springer LNCS 174 (1984).

[NO 87a]   M. Navarro, F. Orejas: On contextual rewriting. *Proc. LANFOR '87*, Barcelona (1987).

[NO 87b]   M. Navarro, F. Orejas: Parameterized Horn clause specifications: proof theory and correctness. *Proc. Joint Conf. on Theory and Practice of Software Development*, Pisa. Springer LNCS 250, 202-216 (1987).

[NO 88]   P. Nivela, F. Orejas: Initial behaviour semantics for algebraic specifications. *Recent Trends in Data Type Specification, Selected Papers from the 5th Workshop on Specification of Abstract Data Types*, Gullane, Scotland. Springer LNCS 332, 184–207 (1988).

[NO 89]   R. Nieuwenhuis, F. Orejas: Clausal completion. Research report LSI-89-29, Universitat Politècnica de Catalunya, Barcelona (1989).

[NUPRL 86]   R.L. Constable, S.F. Allen, H.M. Bromley, W.R. Cleavelend, J.F. Cremer, R.W. Harper, D.J. Howe, T.B. Knoblock, N.P. Mendler, P. Panangaden, J.T. Sasaki, S.F. Smith: *Implementing Mathematics with the Nuprl Proof Development System*. Prentice-Hall (1986).

[NW 83]   T. Nipkow, G. Weikum: A decidability result about sufficient completeness of axiomatically specified abstract data types. *Proc. 6th GI conference on Theoretical Computer Science*. Springer LNCS 145, 257–268 (1983).

[Ore 83]   F. Orejas: Characterizing composability of abstract implementations. *Proc. 1983 Intl. Conf. on Foundations of Computation Theory*, Borgholm, Sweden. Springer LNCS 158 (1983).

[Ore 84]   F. Orejas: A proof system for checking composability of implementations of abstract data types. *Proc. of the Intl. Symp. on Semantics of Data Types*, Sophia-Antipolis. Springer LNCS 173 (1984).

[Ore 85]   F. Orejas: On implementability and computability in abstract data types. In: *Algebra, Logics and Combinatorics in Computer Science*. North-Holland (1985).

[Ore 86]   F. Orejas: The role of abstraction in program development (response). *Proc. IFIP Congress 1986*, Dublin. North-Holland, 143–146 (1986).

[Ore 87a]   F. Orejas: A characterization of passing compatibility for parameterized specifications. *Theoretical Computer Science* 51, 205–214 (1987).

[Ore 87b]   F. Orejas: Theorem proving in conditional equational theories. *Proc. Intl. Workshop on Conditional Term Rewriting*, Orsay. Springer LNCS 308 (1987).

[ONE 89]   F. Orejas, P. Nivela, H. Ehrig: Semantical constructions for categories of behavioural specifications. *Proc Workshop on Categorical Methods in Computer Science with Aspects from Topology*. Springer LNCS 393, 220–241 (1989).

[OSC 89]   F. Orejas, V. Sacristan, S. Clérici: Development of algebraic specifications with constraints. *Proc Workshop on Categorical Methods in Computer Science with Aspects from Topology*. Springer LNCS 393, 102–123 (1989).

[Pad 82]   P. Padawitz: Graph grammars and operational semantics. *Theoretical Computer Science* 19, 117–141 (1982).

[Pad 83]   P. Padawitz: Correctness, Completeness, and Consistency of Equational Data Type Specifications. Ph.D. thesis; Technical Report 83-15, Technische Universität Berlin (1983).

[Pad 84]   P. Padawitz: Towards a proof theory of parameterized specifications. *Proc. of the Intl. Symp. on Semantics of Data Types*, Sophia-Antipolis. Springer LNCS 173, 375–391 (1984).

[Pad 85]   P. Padawitz: Parameter preserving data type specifications. *Proc. Joint Conf. on Theory and Practice of Software Development*, Berlin. Springer LNCS 186, 323–341 (1985).

[Pad 88]   P. Padawitz: *Computing in Horn Clause Theories*. EATCS Monographs on Theoretical Computer Science, Vol. 16. Springer (1988).

[Par 83]   H. Partsch: An exercise in the transformational derivation of an efficient program by joint development of control and data structure. *Science of Computer Programming* 3, 1–35 (1983).

[Par 86]   H. Partsch: Algebraic requirements definition: a case study. *Technology and Science of Informatics* 5(1), 21–36 (1986).

[Par 87]   F. Parisi-Presicce: Partial composition and recursion of module specifications. *Proc. Joint Conf. on Theory and Practice of Software Development*, Pisa. Springer LNCS 249, 217–231 (1987).

[Par 88]   F. Parisi-Presicce: Product and iteration of module specifications. *Proc. 1988 Colloq. on Trees in Algebra and Programming*, Nancy. Springer LNCS 299, 149–164 (1988).

[Par 89]   H. Partsch: Algebraic specification — a step towards future software engineering. *Algebraic Methods: Theory, Tools and Applications.* Springer LNCS 394 (1989).

[Par 90]   H. Partsch: *Specification and Transformation of Programs — A Formal Approach to Software Development.* Springer (1990).

[Pau 84]   E. Paul: Proof by induction in equational theories with relations between constructors. *Proc. 1984 Colloq. on Trees in Algebra and Programming,* Bordeaux. Cambridge University Press, 210–225 (1984).

[Pau 86]   L.C. Paulson: Natural deduction proof as higher-order resolution. *Journal of Logic Programming* 3, 237–258 (1986).

[Pau 87]   L.C. Paulson: *Logic and Computation: Interactive Proof with Cambridge LCF.* Cambridge Univ. Press (1987).

[Pep 79]   P. Pepper: A study on transformational semantics. *Proc. of the International Summer School on Program Construction,* Marktoberdorf. Springer LNCS 69, 322–405 (1979).

[Pep 84a]   P. Pepper: Inferential techniques for program development. *Proc. Workshop on Program Transformations and Programming Environments,* Munich. NATO ASI Series, Vol F8. Springer, 275–290 (1984).

[Pep 84b]   P. Pepper: Algebraic techniques for program specification. *Proc. Workshop on Program Transformations and Programming Environments,* Munich. NATO ASI Series, Vol F8. Springer, 231–244 (1984).

[Pep 87a]   P. Pepper: A simple calculus of program transformations (inclusive of induction). *Science of Computer Programming* 9(3), 221–262 (1987).

[Pep 87b]   P. Pepper: Specification of distributed systems using modal logics. *Proc. GI Arbeitstagung* (1987).

[Per 86]   H. Perdrix: Program synthesis from specifications. *Proc. ESPRIT Conf. '85: Status Report of Continuing Work.* North Holland, 371–385 (1986).

[Pey 87]   S.L. Peyton Jones: *The Implementation of Functional Programming Languages.* Prentice-Hall (1987).

[Pla 78]   D.A. Plaisted: A recursively defined ordering for proving termination of term rewriting systems. Report R-78-943, Univ. of Illinois (1978).

[Pla 82]   D.A. Plaisted: An initial algebra semantics for error presentations. Unpublished Draft (1982).

[Pla 85]   D.A. Plaisted: Semantic confluence tests and completion methods. *Information and Control* 65(2&3), 182–215 (1985).

[Pla 86]   D.A. Plaisted: A simple non-termination test for the Knuth-Bendix method. *Proc. 8th Conf. on Automated Deduction*, Oxford. Springer LNCS 230, 79–88 (1986).

[Plo 72]   G.D. Plotkin: Building-in equational theories. *Machine Intelligence 7*, 73–90 (1972).

[Poi 86]   A. Poigné: Parameterisation for order-sorted algebraic specifications. Technical Report, Imperial College, London (1986).

[Pue 86]   L. Puel: Using unavoidable sets of trees to generalize Kruskal's theorem. Report 86-4, Laboratoire d'Informatique de la Ecole Normale Superieure, Paris (1986).

[Pue 87]   L. Puel: Bon préordres sur les arbres associés à des ensembles inévitables et preuves de terminaison de systèmes de réécriture. Thèse d'Etat, Université Paris VII (1987).

[Pue 89]   L. Puel: Embedding with patterns and associated recursive path ordering. *Proc. 3rd Conf. on Rewriting Techniques and Applications*, Chapel Hill, North Carolina. Springer LNCS 355, 371–387 (1989).

[PA 89]   R. Peña, L.M. Alonso: Specification and verification of TCSP systems by means of partial abstract data types. *Proc. Joint Conf. on Theory and Practice of Software Development*, Barcelona. Springer LNCS 351, 328–344 (1989).

[PB 79]   H. Partsch, M. Broy: Examples for changes of types and object structures. *Proc. of the International Summer School on Program Construction*, Marktoberdorf. Springer LNCS 69, 421–463 (1979).

[PEE 81]   U. Pletat, G. Engels, H.-D. Ehrich: Operational semantics of algebraic specifications with conditional equations. Report 118, Universität Dortmund (1981).

[PL 82]   H. Partsch, A. Laut: From requirements of their formalization — a case study on the stepwise development of algebraic specifications. *Proc. 7. Fachtagung Programmiersprachen und Programmentwicklung*, München 1982. Springer IFB 53, 117–132 (1982).

[PP 83]   H. Partsch, P. Pepper: Abstract data types as a tool for requirements engineering. In: *Requirements Engineering* (D. Kroenig and G. Hommel, eds.). Springer IFB 74, 42–55 (1983).

[PP 86]   H. Partsch, P. Pepper: Program transformations expressed by algebraic type manipulations. *Technology and Science of Informatics* 5(3), 197–212 (1986).

[Qia 89]   Z. Qian: Relation-sorted algebraic specifications with built-in coercers: parameterization and parameter passing. *Proc Workshop on Categorical*

Methods in Computer Science with Aspects from Topology. Springer LNCS 393, 244–260 (1989).

[Qia 90]   Z. Qian: Higher-order order-sorted algebras. *Proc. 2nd Intl. Conf. on Algebraic and Logic Programming*, Nancy. Springer LNCS (1990).

[Rao 84]   J.C. Raoult: On Graph Rewritings. *Theoretical Computer Science* 32, 1–24 (1984).

[Rei 80]   H. Reichel: Initially restricting algebraic theories. *Proc. 1980 Symp. on Mathematical Foundations of Computer Science*. Springer LNCS 88, 504–514 (1980).

[Rei 81]   H. Reichel: Behavioural equivalence — a unifying concept for initial and final specification methods. *Proc. 3rd. Hungarian Comp. Sci. Conference*, 27–39 (1981).

[Rei 85]   H. Reichel: Behavioural validity of equations in abstract data types. *Proc. of the Vienna Conference on Contributions to General Algebra*. Teubner-Verlag, 301–324 (1985).

[Rei 87]   H. Reichel: *Initial Computability, Algebraic Specifications, and Partial Algebras*. Oxford Univ. Press (1987).

[Rem 82]   J.L. Rémy: Etude des systèmes de réécriture conditionnels et applications aux types abstraits algébriques. Thèse d'Etat, Nancy (1982).

[Ret 87]   P. Rety: Improving basic narrowing. *Proc. 2nd Conf. on Rewriting Techniques and Applications*, Bordeaux. Springer LNCS 256 (1987).

[Reu 90]   B. Reus: Algebraische Spezifikation mit Funktionen höherer Ordnung. Diplomarbeit, Universität Passau (1990).

[Rob 65]   J. A. Robinson: A machine-oriented logic based on the resolution principle. *Journal of the Assoc. for Computing Machinery* 12 (1965).

[Rob 85]   P. Robinson: The sum: an AI coprocessor. *Byte* 10(6) (1987).

[Rus 87a]   M. Rusinowitch: Path of subterm ordering and recursive decomposition ordering revisited. *Journal of Symbolic Computation* 3(1&2), 117–132 (1987).

[Rus 87b]   M. Rusinowitch: Theorem-proving with resolution and superposition: an extension of Knuth and Bendix procedure as a complete set of inference rules. Report 87-R-128, CRIN, Nancy (1987).

[Rus 87c]   M. Rusinowitch: On termination of the direct sum of term rewriting systems. *Information Processing Letters* 26(2), 65–70 (1987).

[RKKL 85]   P. Rety, C. Kirchner, H. Kirchner, P. Lescanne: Narrower: a new al-
              gorithm for unification and its application to logic programming. *Proc.*
              Conf. on Rewriting Techniques and Applications, Dijon. Springer LNCS
              202, 141–157 (1985).

[RZ 84]   J.L. Rémy, H. Zhang: REVEUR4: A system for validating conditional
              algebraic specifications of abstract data types. *Proc. 5th European Conf.*
              on Artificial Intelligence, Pisa (1984).

[San 84]   D.T. Sannella: A set-theoretic semantics for CLEAR. *Acta Informatica*
              21, 443–472 (1984).

[Sat 79]   M. Sato: Towards a mathematical theory of program synthesis. *Proc. 6th*
              Intl. Joint Conf. on Artificial Intelligence, Tokyo, 757–762 (1979).

[Sch 77]   K. Schutte: *Proof Theory.* Springer (1977).

[Sch 86a]   M. Schmidt-Schauss: Unification in many sorted equational theories. *Proc.*
              8th Conf. on Automated Deduction, Oxford. Springer LNCS 230 (1986).

[Sch 86b]   K. Schmucker: MacApp: an application framework. *Byte* 11(8), 189–193
              (1986).

[Sch 87a]   M. Schmidt-Schauss: Unification in a combination of arbitrary disjoint
              equational theories. Technical Report, Universität Kaiserslautern (1987).

[Sch 87b]   O. Schoett: Data Abstraction and the Correctness of Modular Program-
              ming. Ph.D. thesis; Report CST-42-87, Dept. of Computer Science, Univ.
              of Edinburgh (1987).

[Sch 90]   O. Schoett: Behavioural correctness of data representations. *Science of*
              Computer Programming 14, 43–57 (1990).

[Sco 82]   D.S. Scott: Domains for denotational semantics. *Proc. 9th Intl. Colloq.*
              on Automata, Languages and Programming, Aarhus. Springer LNCS 140,
              577–613 (1982).

[Sha 86]   N. Shankar: Proof Checking Metamathematics. Ph.D. thesis, Univ. of
              Texas, Austin (1986).

[Sie 89]   J. Siekmann: Unification theory. *Journal of Symbolic Computation*, to
              appear.

[Sin 87]   M. Sintzoff: Expressing program developments in a design calculus. *Proc.*
              of the International Summer School on Logic of Programming and Calculi
              of Discrete Design, Marktoberdorf. Nato ASI Series, Vol. F36. Springer,
              343–365 (1987).

[Smi 85]   R.D. Smith: Top-down synthesis of simple divide and conquer algorithms.
              Artificial Intelligence 27(1), 43–96 (1985).

94

[Sta 80]   J. Staples: Computation on graph-like expressions. *Theoretical Computer Science* 10, 171–185 (1980).

[Ste 82]   R. Steinbrüggen: Program development using transformational expressions. Report TUM-I8206, Technische Universität München (1982).

[Sti 75]   M.E. Stickel: A complete unification algorithm for associative-commutative functions. *Proc. 8th Intl. Joint Conf. on Artificial Intelligence*, Tbilissi (1975).

[Sti 81]   M.E. Stickel: A unification algorithm for associative-commutative functions. *Journal of the Assoc. for Computing Machinery* 28, 423–434 (1981).

[Sti 86]   M. Stickel: A PROLOG technology theorem prover: implementation by an extended PROLOG compiler. *Proc. 8th Conf. on Automated Deduction*, Oxford. Springer LNCS 230, 573–587 (1986).

[Sub 81]   P.A. Subrahmanyam: Nondeterminism in abstract data types. *Proc. 8th Intl. Colloq. on Automata, Languages and Programming*. Springer LNCS 115, 148–164 (1981).

[Swa 82]   W. Swartout: GIST english generator. *Proc. of American Assoc. for Artificial Intelligence* (1982).

[Sza 79]   P. Szabo: The undecidability of the DA-unification problem. Technical Report, Universität Karlsruhe (1979).

[SB 83]   D.T. Sannella, R.M. Burstall: Structured theories in LCF. *Proc. 1983 Colloq. on Trees in Algebra and Programming*, L'Aquila. Springer LNCS 159, 377–391 (1983).

[SD 87]   G. Sivakumar, N. Dershowitz: Goal directed equation solving. Technical Report, Univ. of Illinois at Urbana-Champaign (1987).

[SFSE 89]   A. Sernadas, J. Fiadeiro, C. Sernadas, H.-D. Ehrich: Abstract object types: a temporal perspective. *Proc. Colloq. on Temporal Logic and Specification*. Springer LNCS, to appear.

[SM 87]   K. Subieta, M. Missala: Denotational semantics of query languages. *Information Systems* 12 (1987).

[SNGM 89]   G. Smolka, W. Nutt, J.A. Goguen, J. Meseguer: Order sorted equational computation. *Proc. Colloq. on Resolution of Equations in Algebraic Structures*, Austin. Academic Press (1989).

[SS 82]   J. Siekmann, P. Szabo: Universal unification and classification of equational theories. *Proc. 6th Conf. on Automated Deduction*. Springer LNCS 138 (1982).

[SS 83]   W.L. Scherlis and D.S. Scott: First steps towards inferential programming. *Proc. IFIP Congress 1983*. North-Holland, 199–212 (1983).

[SS 84]   J. Siekmann, P. Szabo: Universal unification. *Proc. 7th Conf. on Automated Deduction.* Springer LNCS 170, 1–42 (1984).

[SS 85]   A. Sernadas, C. Sernadas: The use of ER abstractions in knowledge representation. In: *Entity Relationship Approach: The Use of ER Concept in Knowledge Representation* (P. Chen, ed.). North-Holland, 224–231 (1985).

[SS 87]   A. Sernadas, C. Sernadas: Conceptual modeling for knowledge-based DSS development. In: *Decision Support Systems: Theory and Application* (C. Holsapple and A. Whinston, eds.). Springer, 91–135 (1987).

[SSE 87]   A. Sernadas, C. Sernadas, H.-D. Ehrich: Object-oriented specification of databases: an algebraic approach. *Proc. 13th Int. Conf. on Very Large Data Bases.* Morgan Kaufmann, 107–116 (1987).

[ST 84]   D.T. Sannella, A. Tarlecki: Building specifications in an arbitrary institution. *Proc. of the Intl. Symp. on Semantics of Data Types*, Sophia-Antipolis. Springer LNCS 173, 337–356 (1984).

[ST 85]   D.T. Sannella, A. Tarlecki: Program specification and development in Standard ML. *Proc. 12th ACM Symp. on Principles of Programming Languages*, New Orleans, 67–77 (1985).

[ST 86]   D.T. Sannella, A. Tarlecki: Extended ML: an institution-independent framework for formal program development. *Proc. Workshop on Category Theory and Computer Programming*, Guildford. Springer LNCS 240, 364–389 (1986).

[ST 87a]   D.T. Sannella, A. Tarlecki: On observational equivalence and algebraic specification. *Journal of Computer and System Sciences* 34, 150–178 (1987).

[ST 87b]   D.T. Sannella, A. Tarlecki: Toward formal development of programs from algebraic specifications: implementations revisited. Extended abstract in: *Proc. Joint Conf. on Theory and Practice of Software Development*, Pisa. Springer LNCS 249, 96–110 (1987); full version in *Acta Informatica* 25, 233–281 (1988).

[ST 88a]   D.T. Sannella, A. Tarlecki: Specifications in an arbitrary institution. *Information and Computation* 76, 165–210 (1988).

[ST 88b]   D.T. Sannella, A. Tarlecki (eds.): *Recent Trends in Data Type Specification, Selected Papers from the 5th Workshop on Specification of Abstract Data Types*, Gullane, Scotland. Springer LNCS 332 (1988).

[ST 89]   D.T. Sannella, A. Tarlecki: Toward formal development of ML programs: foundations and methodology. *Proc. Joint Conf. on Theory and Practice of Software Development*, Barcelona. Springer LNCS 352, 375–389 (1989).

[STW 87]   P. Schmitz, M. Timm, M. Windfuhr (eds.): *Requirements Engineering '87.* GMD-Studien 121 (1987).

[SW 82]   D.T. Sannella, M. Wirsing: Implementation of parameterised specifica-
            tions. *Proc. 9th Intl. Colloq. on Automata, Languages and Programming*,
            Aarhus. Springer LNCS 140, 473–488 (1982).

[SW 83]   D.T. Sannella, M. Wirsing: A kernel language for algebraic specification
            and implementation. *Proc. 1983 Intl. Conf. on Foundations of Computa-
            tion Theory*, Borgholm, Sweden. Springer LNCS 158, 413–427 (1983).

[SW 87]   D.T. Sannella, L.A. Wallen: A calculus for the construction of modular
            Prolog programs. *Proc. 1987 IEEE Symp. on Logic Programming*, San
            Francisco, 368–378 (1987).

[Tar 85]   A. Tarlecki: Bits and pieces of the theory of institutions. *Proc. Workshop
            on Category Theory and Computer Programming*, Guildford. Springer
            LNCS 240, 334–363 (1986).

[Tar 86a]   A. Tarlecki: On the existence of free models in abstract algebraic institu-
            tions. *Theoretical Computer Science* 37, 269–304 (1986).

[Tar 86b]   A. Tarlecki: Quasi-varieties in abstract algebraic institutions. *Journal of
            Computer and System Sciences* 33, 333–360 (1986).

[Thi 84]   J.-J. Thiel: Stop losing sleep over incomplete data type specifications.
            Proc. 11th ACM Symp. on Principles of Programming Languages (1984).

[Tid 86]   E. Tiden: Unification in combinations of collapse-free theories with dis-
            joint sets of functions symbols. *Proc. 8th Conf. on Automated Deduction*,
            Oxford. Springer LNCS 230, 431–449 (1986).

[Toy 87]   Y. Toyama: Counterexamples to termination of the direct sum of term
            rewriting systems. *Information Processing Letters* 25(3), 141–143 (1987).

[TKB 89]   Y. Toyama, J.W. Klop, H.P. Barendregt: Termination for the direct sum
            of left-linear term rewriting systems. *Proc. 3rd Conf. on Rewriting Tech-
            niques and Applications*, Chapel Hill, North Carolina. Springer LNCS 355
            (1989).

[TW 86]   A. Tarlecki, M. Wirsing: Continuous abstract data types. *Fundamenta
            Informaticae* 9, 95–125 (1986).

[TWW 78]   J.W. Thatcher, E.G. Wagner, J.B. Wright: Data type specification: pa-
            rameterization and the power of specification techniques. *SIGACT 10th
            Annual Symp. on the Theory of Computing*, San Diego (1978). Also in:
            ACM Trans. on Programming Languages and Systems 4, 711–773 (1982).

[TWW 79]   J.W. Thatcher, E.G. Wagner, J.B. Wright: More on advice on structuring
            compilers and proving them correct. *Proc. 6th Intl. Colloq. on Automata,
            Languages and Programming*. Springer LNCS 71, 596–615 (1979). *Theo-
            retical Computer Science* 15, 223–250 (1981).

[Voi 86]   F. Voisin: CIGALE: a tool for interactive grammar construction and ex-
             pression parsing. *Science of Computer Programming* 7(1), 61–86 (1986).

[Wal 84]   C. Walther: Unification in many sorted theories. *Proc. 5th European Conf.
             on Artificial Intelligence*, Pisa. ECAI, 593–602 (1984).

[Wal 89]   U. Waldmann: Semantics of order-sorted specifications. Report 297, Uni-
             versität Dortmund (1989); *Theoretical Computer Science*, to appear.

[Wan 79]   M. Wand: Final algebra semantics and data type extensions. *Journal of
             Computer and System Sciences* 19, 27–44 (1979).

[Wan 80]   M. Wand: First-order identites as a defining language. *Acta Informatica*
             14, 337–357 (1980).

[War 77]   D.H.D. Warren: Implementing Prolog: compiling predicate logic pro-
             grams. Reports DAI-39 and DAI-40, Univ. of Edinburgh (1977).

[Wil 86]   D. Wile: Program developments: formal explanations of implementations.
             Comm. of the Assoc. for Computing Machinery 26(11), 902–911 (1983);
             also in: *New Paradigms for Software Development* (W.A. Agresti, ed.).
             IEEE Computer Society Press/North Holland, 239–248 (1986).

[Win 89]   J.M. Wing: Specifying Avalon objects in Larch. *Proc. Joint Conf. on
             Theory and Practice of Software Development*, Barcelona. Springer LNCS
             352, 61–80 (1989).

[Wir 86]   M. Wirsing: Structured algebraic specifications: a kernel language. *Theo-
             retical Computer Science* 42, 123–249 (1986).

[Wir 88]   M. Wirsing: Algebraic description of reusable software components. *COM-
             PEURO '88* (1988).

[Wir 90]   M. Wirsing: Algebraic specification. In: *Handbook of Theoretical Com-
             puter Science* (J. van Leeuwen, ed.). North-Holland (1990).

[Wol 87]   M. Wolczko: Semantics of Smalltalk-80. *Proc. 1987 European Conf. on
             Object Oriented Programming*. Springer LNCS 276 (1987).

[WB 82]   M. Wirsing, M. Broy: An analysis of semantic models for algebraic spec-
             ifications. *Proc. Intl. Summer School on Theoretical Foundations of Pro-
             gramming Methodology*, Marktoberdorf. Reidel (1982).

[WB 89a]   D. Wolz, P. Boehm: Compilation of LOTOS data type specifications.
             Proc. 9th Int. Symp. on Protocol Specification, Testing, and Verification,
             Enschede (1989).

[WB 89b]   M. Wirsing, M. Broy: A modular framework for specification and imple-
             mentation. *Proc. Joint Conf. on Theory and Practice of Software Devel-
             opment*, Barcelona. Springer LNCS 351, 42–73 (1989).

[WB 89c]   M. Wirsing, J.A. Bergstra: *Algebraic Methods: Theory, Tools and Applications*. Springer LNCS 394 (1989).

[WE 86]   H. Weber, H. Ehrig: Specification of modular systems. *IEEE Trans. on Software Engineering* SE-12(7), 784–798 (1986).

[WE 87]   E.G. Wagner, H. Ehrig: Canonical constraints for parameterized data types. *Theoretical Computer Science* 30, 323–351 (1987).

[WE 88]   H. Weber, H. Ehrig: Specification of concurrently executable modules and distributed modular systems. *Proc. Intl. Workshop on the Future Trends of Distributed Computing Systems in the 1990's*, Hong Kong, 202–215 (1988).

[WHS 89]   M. Wirsing, R. Hennicker, R. Stabl. Menu: an example for the systematic reuse of specifications. *Proc. 2nd European Conf. on Software Engineering.* Springer LNCS 387, 20-41 (1989).

[WPPDB 83]   M. Wirsing, P. Pepper, H. Partsch, W. Dosch, M. Broy: On hierarchies of abstract data types. *Acta Informatica* 20, 1–33 (1983).

[Yel 85]   K. Yellick: Combining unification algorithm for confined equational theories. *Proc. Conf. on Rewriting Techniques and Applications*, Dijon. Springer LNCS 202, 301–324 (1985).

[Zil 74]   S.N. Zilles: Algebraic specification of abstract data types. Computation Structures Group memo 119, Laboratory for Computer Science, MIT (1974).

[ZR 85]   H. Zhang, J.L. Rémy: Contextual rewriting. *Proc. Conf. on Rewriting Techniques and Applications*, Dijon. Springer LNCS 202 (1985).

Lecture Notes in Computer Science

For information about Vols. 1–420
please contact your bookseller or Springer-Verlag

Vol. 421: T. Onodera, S. Kawai, A Formal Model of Visualization in Computer Graphics Systems. X, 100 pages. 1990.

Vol. 422: B. Nebel, Reasoning and Revision in Hybrid Representation Systems. XII, 270 pages. 1990 (Subseries LNAI).

Vol. 423: L.E. Deimel (Ed.), Software Engineering Education. Proceedings, 1990. VI, 164 pages. 1990.

Vol. 424: G. Rozenberg (Ed.), Advances in Petri Nets 1989. VI, 524 pages. 1990.

Vol. 425: C.H. Bergman, R.D. Maddux, D.L. Pigozzi (Eds.), Algebraic Logic and Universal Algebra in Computer Science. Proceedings, 1988. XI, 292 pages. 1990.

Vol. 426: N. Houbak, SIL – a Simulation Language. VII, 192 pages. 1990.

Vol. 427: O. Faugeras (Ed.), Computer Vision – ECCV 90. Proceedings, 1990. XII, 619 pages. 1990.

Vol. 428: D. Bjørner, C.A.R. Hoare, H. Langmaack (Eds.), VDM '90. VDM and Z – Formal Methods in Software Development. Proceedings, 1990. XVII, 580 pages. 1990.

Vol. 429: A. Miola (Ed.), Design and Implementation of Symbolic Computation Systems. Proceedings, 1990. XII, 284 pages. 1990.

Vol. 430: J.W. de Bakker, W.-P. de Roever, G. Rozenberg (Eds.), Stepwise Refinement of Distributed Systems. Models, Formalisms, Correctness. Proceedings, 1989. X, 808 pages. 1990.

Vol. 431: A. Arnold (Ed.), CAAP '90. Proceedings, 1990. VI, 285 pages. 1990.

Vol. 432: N. Jones (Ed.), ESOP '90. Proceedings, 1990. IX, 436 pages. 1990.

Vol. 433: W. Schröder-Preikschat, W. Zimmer (Eds.), Progress in Distributed Operating Systems and Distributed Systems Management. Proceedings, 1989. V, 206 pages. 1990.

Vol. 434: J.-J. Quisquater, J. Vandewalle (Eds.), Advances in Cryptology – EUROCRYPT '89. Proceedings, 1989. X, 710 pages. 1990.

Vol. 435: G. Brassard (Ed.), Advances in Cryptology – CRYPTO '89. Proceedings, 1989. XIII, 634 pages. 1990.

Vol. 436: B. Steinholtz, A. Sølvberg, L. Bergman (Eds.), Advanced Information Systems Engineering. Proceedings, 1990. X, 392 pages. 1990.

Vol. 437: D. Kumar (Ed.), Current Trends in SNePS – Semantic Network Processing System. Proceedings, 1989. VII, 162 pages. 1990. (Subseries LNAI).

Vol. 438: D.H. Norrie, H.W. Six (Eds.), Computer Assisted Learning – ICCAL '90. Proceedings, 1990. VII, 467 pages. 1990.

Vol. 439: P. Gorny, M. Tauber (Eds.), Visualization in Human-Computer Interaction. Proceedings, 1988. VI, 274 pages. 1990.

Vol. 440: E. Börger, H. Kleine Büning, M.M. Richter (Eds.), CSL '89. Proceedings, 1989. VI, 437 pages. 1990.

Vol. 441: T. Ito, R.H. Halstead, Jr. (Eds.), Parallel Lisp: Languages and Systems. Proceedings, 1989. XII, 364 pages. 1990.

Vol. 442: M. Main, A. Melton, M. Mislove, D. Schmidt (Eds.), Mathematical Foundations of Programming Semantics. Proceedings, 1989. VI, 439 pages. 1990.

Vol. 443: M.S. Paterson (Ed.), Automata, Languages and Programming. Proceedings, 1990. IX, 781 pages. 1990.

Vol. 444: S. Ramani, R. Chandrasekar, K.S.R. Anjaneyulu (Eds.), Knowledge Based Computer Systems. Proceedings, 1989. X, 546 pages. 1990. (Subseries LNAI).

Vol. 445: A.J.M. van Gasteren, On the Shape of Mathematical Arguments. VIII, 181 pages. 1990.

Vol. 446: L. Plümer, Termination Proofs for Logic Programs. VIII ,142 pages. 1990. (Subseries LNAI).

Vol. 447: J.R. Gilbert, R. Karlsson (Eds.), SWAT '90. 2nd Scandinavian Workshop on Algorithm Theory. Proceedings, 1990. VI, 417 pages. 1990.

Vol. 448: B. Simons, A. Spector (Eds.), Fault Tolerant Distributed Computing. VI, 298 pages. 1990.

Vol. 449: M.E. Stickel (Ed.), 10th International Conference on Automated Deduction. Proceedings, 1990. XVI, 688 pages. 1990. (Subseries LNAI).

Vol. 450: T. Asano, T. Ibaraki, H. Imai, T. Nishizeki (Eds.), Algorithms. Proceedings, 1990. VIII, 479 pages. 1990.

Vol. 451: V. Mařík, O. Stepánková, Z. Zdráhal (Eds.), Artificial Intelligence in Higher Education. Proceedings, 1989. IX, 247 pages. 1990. (Subseries LNAI).

Vol. 452: B. Rovan (Ed.), Mathematical Foundations of Computer Science 1990. Proceedings, 1990. VIII, 544 pages. 1990.

Vol. 453: J. Seberry, J. Pieprzyk (Eds.), Advances in Cryptology – AUSCRYPT '90 Proceedings, 1990. IX. 462 pages. 1990.

Vol. 454: V. Diekert, Combinatorics on Traces. XII, 165 pages. 1990.

Vol. 455: C.A. Floudas, P.M. Pardalos, A Collection of Test Problems for Constrained Global Optimization Algorithms. XIV, 180 pages. 1990.

Vol. 456: P. Deransart, J. Maluszyn'ski (Eds.), Programming Language Implementation and Logic Programming. Proceedings, 1990. VIII, 401 pages. 1990.

Vol. 457: H. Burkhart (Ed.), CONPAR '90 – VAPP IV. Proceedings, 1990. XIV, 900 pages. 1990.

Vol. 458: J.C.M. Baeten, J.W. Klop (Eds.), CONCUR '90. Proceedings, 1990. VII, 537 pages. 1990.

Vol. 459: R. Studer (Ed.), Natural Language and Logic. Proceedings, 1989. VII, 252 pages. 1990. (Subseries LNAI).

Vol. 460: J. Uhl, H.A. Schmid, A Systematic Catalogue of Reusable Abstract Data Types. XII, 344 pages. 1990.

Vol. 461: P. Deransart, M. Jourdan (Eds.), Attribute Grammars and their Applications. Proceedings, 1990. VIII, 358 pages. 1990.

Vol. 462: G. Gottlob, W. Nejdl (Eds.), Expert Systems in Engineering. Proceedings, 1990. IX, 260 pages. 1990. (Subseries LNAI).

Vol. 463: H. Kirchner, W. Wechler (Eds.), Algebraic and Logic Programming. Proceedings, 1990. VII, 386 pages. 1990.

Vol. 464: J. Dassow, J. Kelemen (Eds.), Aspects and Prospects of Theoretical Computer Science. Proceedings, 1990. VI, 298 pages. 1990.

Vol. 465: A. Fuhrmann, M. Morreau (Eds.), The Logic of Theory Change. Proceedings, 1989. X, 334 pages. 1991. (Subseries LNAI).

Vol. 466: A. Blaser (Ed.), Database Systems of the 90s. Proceedings, 1990. VIII, 334 pages. 1990.

Vol. 467: F. Long (Ed.), Software Engineering Environments. Proceedings, 1969. VI, 313 pages. 1990.

Vol. 468: S.G. Akl, F. Fiala, W.W. Koczkodaj (Eds.), Advances in Computing and Information – ICCI '90. Proceedings, 1990. VII, 529 pages. 1990.

Vol. 469: I. Guessarian (Ed.), Semantics of Systeme of Concurrent Processes. Proceedings, 1990. V, 456 pages. 1990.

Vol. 470: S. Abiteboul, P.C. Kanellakis (Eds.), ICDT '90. Proceedings, 1990. VII, 528 pages. 1990.

Vol. 471: B.C. Ooi, Efficient Query Processing in Geographic Information Systems. VIII, 208 pages. 1990.

Vol. 472: K.V. Nori, C.E. Veni Madhavan (Eds.), Foundations of Software Technology and Theoretical Computer Science. Proceedings, 1990. X, 420 pages. 1990.

Vol. 473: I.B. Damgård (Ed.), Advances in Cryptology – EUROCRYPT '90. Proceedings, 1990. VIII, 500 pages. 1991.

Vol. 474: D. Karagiannis (Ed.), Information Syetems and Artificial Intelligence: Integration Aspects. Proceedings, 1990. X, 293 pages. 1991. (Subseries LNAI).

Vol. 475: P. Schroeder-Heister (Ed.), Extensions of Logic Programming. Proceedings, 1989. VIII, 364 pages. 1991. (Subseries LNAI).

Vol. 476: M. Filgueiras, L. Damas, N. Moreira, A.P. Tomás (Eds.), Natural Language Processing. Proceedings, 1990. VII, 253 pages. 1991. (Subseries LNAI).

Vol. 477: D. Hammer (Ed.), Compiler Compilers. Proceedings, 1990. VI, 227 pages. 1991.

Vol. 478: J. van Eijck (Ed.), Logics in AI. Proceedings, 1990. IX, 562 pages. 1991. (Subseries in LNAI).

Vol. 480: C. Choffrut, M. Jantzen (Eds.), STACS 91. Proceedings, 1991. X, 549 pages. 1991.

Vol. 481: E. Lang, K.-U. Carstensen, G. Simmons, Modelling Spatial Knowledge on a Linguistic Basis. IX, 138 pages. 1991. (Subseries LNAI).

Vol. 482: Y. Kodratoff (Ed.), Machine Learning – EWSL-91. Proceedings, 1991. XI, 537 pages. 1991. (Subseries LNAI).

Vol. 483: G. Rozenberg (Ed.), Advances In Petri Nets 1990. VI, 515 pages. 1991.

Vol. 484: R. H. Möhring (Ed.), Graph-Theoretic Concepts In Computer Science. Proceedings, 1990. IX, 360 pages. 1991.

Vol. 485: K. Furukawa, H. Tanaka, T. Fullsaki (Eds.), Logic Programming '89. Proceedings, 1989. IX, 183 pages. 1991. (Subseries LNAI).

Vol. 486: J. van Leeuwen, N. Santoro (Eds.), Distributed Algorithms. Proceedings, 1990. VI, 433 pages. 1991.

Vol. 487: A. Bode (Ed.), Distributed Memory Computing. Proceedings, 1991. XI, 506 pages. 1991.

Vol. 488: R. V. Book (Ed.), Rewriting Techniques and Applications. Proceedings, 1991. VII, 458 pages. 1991.

Vol. 489: J. W. de Bakker, W. P. de Roever, G. Rozenberg (Eds.), Foundations of Object-Oriented Languages. Proceedings, 1990. VIII, 442 pages. 1991.

Vol. 490: J. A. Bergstra, L. M. G. Feljs (Eds.), Algebraic Methods 11: Theory, Tools and Applications. VI, 434 pages. 1991.

Vol. 491: A. Yonezawa, T. Ito (Eds.), Concurrency: Theory, Language, and Architecture. Proceedings, 1989. VIII, 339 pages. 1991.

Vol. 492: D. Sriram, R. Logcher, S. Fukuda (Eds.), Computer-Aided Cooperative Product Development. Proceedings, 1989 VII, 630 pages. 1991.

Vol. 493: S. Abramsky, T. S. E. Maibaum (Eds.), TAPSOFT '91. Volume 1. Proceedings, 1991. VIII, 455 pages. 1991.

Vol. 494: S. Abramsky, T. S. E. Maibaum (Eds.), TAPSOFT '91. Volume 2. Proceedings, 1991. VIII, 482 pages. 1991.

Vol. 495: 9. Thalheim, J. Demetrovics, H.-D. Gerhardt (Eds.), MFDBS '91. Proceedings, 1991. VI, 395 pages. 1991.

Vol. 496: H.-P. Schwefel, R. Männer (Eds.), Parallel Problem Solving from Nature. Proceedings, 1991. XI, 485 pages. 1991.

Vol. 497: F. Dehne, F. Fiala. W.W. Koczkodaj (Eds.), Advances in Computing and Intormation - ICCI '91 Proceedings, 1991. VIII, 745 pages. 1991.

Vol. 498: R. Andersen, J. A. Bubenko jr., A. Sølvberg (Eds.), Advanced Information Systems Engineering. Proceedings, 1991. VI, 579 pages. 1991.

Vol. 499: D. Christodoulakis (Ed.), Ada: The Choice for '92. Proceedings, 1991. VI, 411 pages. 1991.

Vol. 500: M. Held, On the Computational Geometry of Pocket Machining. XII, 179 pages. 1991.

Vol. 501: M. Bidoit, H.-J. Kreowski, P. Lescanne, F. Orejas, D. Sannella (Eds.), Algebraic System Specification and Development. VIII, 98 pages. 1991.